Song for Almeyda and Song for Anninho

ALSO BY GAYL JONES

Fiction

Corregidora (novel) (1975)

Eva's Man (novel) (1976)

White Rat (short stories) (1977)

The Healing (novel) (1998)

Mosquito (novel) (1999)

Palmares (novel) (2021)

Poetry collections

Song for Anninho (1981)

The Hermit-Woman (1983)

Xarque and Other Poems (1985)

Other works

Chile Woman (play) (1974)

Liberating Voices:
Oral Tradition in African American Literature
(criticism) (1991)

SONG FOR ALMEYDA
&
SONG FOR ANNINHO

GAYL JONES

BEACON PRESS
BOSTON, MA

Beacon Press
Boston, Massachusetts
www.beacon.org

Beacon Press books
are published under the auspices of
the Unitarian Universalist Association of Congregations.

25 24 23 22   8 7 6 5 4 3 2 1

This book is printed on acid-free paper that meets the uncoated paper
ANSI/NISO specifications for permanence as revised in 1992.

Text design by Nancy Koerner at
Wilsted & Taylor Publishing Services

Library of Congress Cataloging-in-Publication Data

Names: Jones, Gayl, author. | Jones, Gayl. Song for Almeyda. |
    Jones, Gayl. Song for Anninho.
Title: Song for Almeyda ; and, Song for Anninho / by Gayl Jones.
Other titles: Song for Anninho
Description: Boston, MA : Beacon Press, [2022] |
    Summary: "Two epic poems, the love songs of fugitive slaves,
    set in 17th-century Brazil"—Provided by publisher.
Identifiers: LCCN 2021042517 | ISBN 9780807029909 (hardback ;
    acid-free paper) | ISBN 9780807029923 (ebook)
Subjects: LCGFT: Poetry.
Classification: LCC PS3560.O483 S58 2022 | DDC 811/.54—dc23
LC record available at https://lccn.loc.gov/2021042517

It is indeed true that the force and stronghold of the Negroes of Palmares located in the famous Barriga range is conquered . . . and that their king was killed (by a party of men from the regiment of the petitioner, which came upon the said King Zumbi on the twentieth of November, 1695) and the survivors scattered. Yet one should not therefore think that this war is ended. No doubt it is close to being terminated if we continue to hunt these survivors through the great depths of these forests, and if the regiment of the petitioners is kept along the frontier. If not, another stronghold will suddenly appear either here in Barriga or in another equally suitable place.

—Petition presented to His Majesty
by Domingos Jorge Velho, "field master"
in the campaign against Palmares, 1695

SONG FOR ALMEYDA

I.

Wise men seek out wise men as if it
were not wise to
        Congregate
        With fools.
You have found your refuge,
          Anninho.
Who are you?
I am Afranio, the curandero. Some
know me as Guerreiro,
        The rubber
        Gatherer.
Others as Anando, the rebel-spy.
But for you I am Afranio,
        The curandero.
You have found your African. You
seek the African in me,
        Eh?
I am part Tupi, part
        African, and
        Part East
        Indian.
You have found your African.
I am descended from high and
        Low.

3

The page of Prince Henry and the
King of the Congo, a Tupi mask
maker
And more rubber gatherers

Than you can count on your fists.
And some say I am descended
From one of
The
Enlightened
Who some say can fly on the
Wings of his
Own virtue.

If you are Afranio, the
Curandero and
Wise man,
Tell me of Almeyda. Is she
Safe?
Did she escape the soldiers?
Did she escape the
Portuguese? Is she safe?

Safe, yes. But first
Questions
First.
Ask first of Zumbi and then
I'll tell you of
your love.

And Zumbi? I know it. He's
                    Immortal him.
                    King Zumbi.
If you are Afranio, the
                    Curandero.
Then you know it too. The

                    Destruction of
                    The old Palmares
Is the spark that builds the
                    New one.

Did I not say that wise men
                    Seek out wise
                    Men first?
But have you been wise to
                    Try to mingle love
and war? You have
                    Found your
                    Refuge,
                    Anninho.
Should I strip you of the
                    Passions?

Of love or war?

The passions of war. For I
                    See a man born
                    Loving.
As I'm one born with a spear

And war paint.
But you have found your
            Africa.
You have found your native
            Country.

This is my native country,
            This Brazil.

I'm an old African, but
            Perhaps you're the
            new.
If so, new men must learn to
            Listen like
            Old ones.
We are descended from high
            And low,
            Anninho.
The page of Prince Henry and the
King of the Congo, a Tupi mask
maker
And more rubber gatherers than you
      can count on your fists
      And some say we're descended
            Even from one of
            the
Enlightened.
Who some say can fly on the
            Wings of his
            Own virtue.

But chew this, Anninho. Your
wounds are not deep, Anninho,
Guerreiro,
So it is the spirit that I
                Heal.

Tell me of Almeyda. First

tell me, Afranio,
Who is this boy who brings
                The brew,

Who brings the manioc cakes
                And rice,
Who brings the guava and
                Pacobas,
And coconut milk to quench
                The thirst, who
is this young boy, Who does
your bidding?

Don't you recognize your
                Younger self? It's
you, your younger self,
                That's who, or
my apprentice, or my
                Disciplined
                Disciple,
But he looks younger than he
                Is,

And he does no one's true
               Bidding but
               His own.
There are only free men
               Here, Anninho,
And free women too.
(Some would say a woman's freer.)
Tell me of Almeyda.

I first saw her in a dream. I was
riding on horseback
               And
She was walking with the
               Wise woman. . . .

Zibatra. . . .

Almeydita, this wise one
               Called her in
the dream,
But when I saw her in the
               World
She was a woman grown,
               Almeyda.

Almeyda, there was such a one
Named Almeida who brought the
Africans here, on the
               Slave ship
From the Guinea coast or the

Island of Sao
Tiago
On the *Legitimo Africano* or
The Marianito,
They're all the same ship,
Eh?
In exchange for Brazil nuts,
Sweet brandy,
And cacao
To show him his new country,
Eh?
To get him educated, eh,
Benedito? A
new immigrant, eh?

There are many Almeidas

And one Almeyda, and that
Name
To me has only one meaning, the one
worthy of loving,
The loving one.

A mulher digna de amar

And the guerreira if it's
The same
Almeyda
I've heard can wield a bow and
pack a musket

Not to mention arquebuses, the
loving warrior women,
                    Eh? The warrior
                    loving Woman,
But every contradiction
                    Comes to the
                    New World.
New immigrants, eh?
Why do you chain them, Xaxa?
Immigrants such as these,
                    Sir, rebel if You
                    let them,
Immigrants such as these
                    Jump ship if
                    You let them
And there's one called "the
                    Enlightened" whom
they swear can fly on
                    The wings

Of his own virtue.
A virtuous African?
A dark enlightened one? Why,
didn't I say that every
                    Contradiction
Comes to the New World? But all
time's one, Anninho. Your
younger self is you.
To get him educated, eh? To
civilize him, eh?

Brazil civilizes Africa?
Why, they're some who'll say that
Africa civilizes Brazil.

Wise men seek out wise men as if it
were not wise to
                    Congregate
                    With fools
Deep in these caverns are
                    The pools that
                    Have the healing
Waters.
Benedito, did I call you
                    Benedito?
It's because you remind me
                    Of Benedito,
The African monk.
They are practical holy men,
                    These monks
For when they've enough gold
                    They use it

Not to buy new monks' robes
                    Or more holy
                    Relics
But to buy the freedom of
                    Others.

No, I'm not a Benedictine
                    Monk,

Though I've spent some time in the
                    Monastery.
Africans have their own
                    Monasteries,
                    You know,
The pretos theirs, the
                    Mestizos
                    Theirs,
The brancos theirs, as if
holiness came in
                    Tints.
No, I'm not a monk
But I've spent some time in
                    The monastery
Recruiting some of the newly
                    Freed men and
                    Women
But that's a tale of Anando,
                    The rebel-spy
And not I, eh?
The Tupi mask maker makes
                    Masks within
                    Masks;
Take off one mask and you

                    Discover another
                    mask.
Peel off Afranio and there's
                    Guerreiro,
Peel off Guerreiro and
                    There's

Anando, eh?
You like these caverns?
Your Palmares
Hides in
The palm forests of Alagoas
And ours—but I
won't tell
You the name of this
Quilombo—we
Hide in these
Caverns.
But there are hegemonic
Games here
Too.
Those rebels who stole their
Own freedom think
themselves superior to those who had
their freedom
Purchased
And the men and women of
Purchased
Freedom
Divide themselves into those
Whose freedom
Was purchased
For them by the Benedictine
Africans

And those who purchased
Their own

Freedom
Themselves
With their own reis.
It's the same community, eh?
We're all
Africans, eh?
Steal your freedom or buy it or
have freedom bought for you,
Freedom is freedom, eh?
Liberdade é liberdade freedom is
freedom, that's
What I say.
Freedom is honey. All
honey is sweet.
And any honey is sweeter than
Blood, eh?
So, one rebel to another, don't
tell me the
Superiority
Of one freedom to another. All
freedom is honey.
Sweet.
Strip to your waist and enter these
streams. Perhaps it's freedom
turned
These
Ordinary waters into
healing ones. Rebel to
rebel,
I'm more curandero than

Rebel
For I have an obsession with
Healing.
An obsessão.
Óleo de amendoim.
We'll rub you down with this oil,
Then tell me more of this
Almeyda,
The woman you look upon with favor.
I look upon all my wives
With favor,
Me,
Com bons olhos,
With good eyes.
Love, eh?
I'm no Portuguese, me. That the
Portuguese hurl
Love lances
And plant
Kisses.
I have nothing to do with
The Europeans, me.
It is only European women
Who can only see
themselves
In kisses. To look upon a
Woman with
Good eyes,
With
Favor, is not that loving?

Oh, you New Africans, what
will your nature be?
Those who enter these caverns must not
only wash the chalk
                    From their
                    Faces
But their spirits too.
You have found your African. The
pool we call Origim,
                    The Source.
Oh, you New Africans, who
will you be?

There will be some who'll
                    Say that Africa
has civilized Brazil.
Tell me about your Almeyda.
Isto cancao e para ela.
Do you have an ear for
                    Music?
Those are the congadas that
                    You hear.
We coronate our Congo King,
                    Like your King
                    Zumbi.
Shall we make our king a
                    Throne?
But there are no Doms here
                    Or Princes
                    Either.

Though we have our High
                    Justices (and Low
                    ones too).

But they'll be those who'll
                    Say that Africa
has civilized Brazil.
Do you see your Almeyda in
                    Your dreams?
She has a good ear for
                    Music, eh?
Ela tem ouvido para música.
But she wants to see herself
                    In kisses. Oh,
you New Africans, who will
you be?
She's straight as the spear
                    She carries. I
like her self-possession
                    Too.
Eh, as for me, I look upon
                    All my wives
                    With favor,
The old ones and the new. And
everyone's a warrior and
                    As self-
                    Possessed as any.
That one my other wives call
                    Orgulhosa, the
                    Haughty one.

I call her wonderful myself. And
that one's too Catolica. We got the
chalk off her
                    Face, but not the
                    Portuguese

Inside the Portuguese. And she
doesn't know the
                    Difference
                    Between
Reisados and congadas. She
celebrates the Epiphany
                    Still.
She thinks that Congo
                    Blood's not
                    Royal.
Call her Branqueamenta and
                    She thinks
                    That's her.
But I'll call her Africana, for
she looks like Africa
                    Herself.
Isto cancao e para ela.
She must learn who she is.

And this one's a woman of
                    Quality,
Though the brancos sold her as if
she were a third-rate
                    Girl.

Oceana I call her,
For when I'm with her, I
turn too playful.
New Worlds demand vigilance. Oh,
you New Africans.
Only when I gather rubber do I
trade with the chalked
                    Faces,
Or trade with traders who

                    Trade with
                    Them,
Otherwise I have nothing to
                    Do with the
                    Chalked faces,
Except when there's freedom to be
                    Purchased or
                    Stolen.
Freedom is freedom.
Liberdade é liberdade
And freedom is sweeter than
                    Honey.
Oh, you New Africans.

I look upon all my wives
                    With favor,
                    Anninho.
The old ones and the new. But one
        good wife's good, eh?
Quatro olhos vêem mais que Dois.

But I call all my wives
                    Wonderful.
Your Almeyda,
She has a good ear for music
                    Too, eh?

But my wives come to the
                    Stream to do
                    Their laundry
And wash their hair.

Women are women. They treat
Origim as if it
                    Were just
ordinary water.
Let me show you other
                    Caverns and other
                    streams.
You Palmaristas hide in the
                    Palm forests but in
a new world such as
                    This one Africans
must hide within.
Deep in these caverns are the
                    Pools that
                    Heal.

Eh, Oceana.
But when I'm with her I
turn too playful.

Come.
Be careful of the caltrops
                Here
And the spears for fences. When
we heard of the
                Destruction of
your Palmares, I, as
                Xingar, leader
of the regiment,
Set out our men and women in search
Of those who escaped. So
you are not the only
                Palmarista

We have brought here, but
                There are
                Others
Some being mended, others
telling their tales to
                Ioio
Our scribe.
He does not write in
                Portuguese
But one of the hidden
                Languages of
the Mende;
In the old world
He used to be a member of a secret
society
Where they used writing,

                    Them,
But as for me,
I am but an Old Griot named
                    Dengue
Who listens well
And remembers what he hears Man-of-
Many-Names
They call me here
Dom So-and-So
If I were Dom Anyone.

In this cavern we
grow cacao.
I'm curing it of swollen-
                    Shoot.
Here everyone drinks
                    Chocolate.

Here Africans are Africans. I can't
speak for others, but I only wish
to be
                    Myself.
Oh, New Africans, Who
will you be?

Oh, novos africanos,

Quem você será?

But come, meet the rebel
Angola and

his wife Cabinda.
You know them, I believe,
As you escaped from the same palm
forest.
Share wild yams with us and
meat.
Fingers will do.
Here, Africans are Africans. The
trickles that form these
         Waters
Come fresh from the Congo,
         Some say,
But Congo or not,
Brazil is not my country,
         Nor am I
         Portuguese,
Africa is my country, my
         Only country.

But it is the New World we are.
The New World that
         Transforms us. We
are New Africans, not old
         Ones.

New Africans, eh? And
         Almeyda?
Cabinda spotted her near the river.
A soldier stood over her
         With a machete or a

broad sword,
But someone grabbed Cabinda. Safe, did

you say?

Safe, yes.

Afranio is not one to doubt,
                    Anninho.
He told me of Cabinda's
                    Safety,
Then his regiment found her
                    And brought
                    Her here.

You are indeed a quilombo, but
none I've heard spoken
                    Of.

It is not good for quilombos
                    To be known.
We keep ourselves hidden in
                    These caverns.
To the Portuguese, we're
                    Simple rubber
                    Gatherers.
And not everyone we rescue,
                    Anninho, finds
their way into these
                    Caverns,

For though all Africans are
                    Africans, not all
Africans are free.
But eat up, my good fellow. We grow
the best yams here. Efo brings Efo.
Is the vatapá too highly
                    Seasoned? Eat up,
my good fellow. Not all Africans
are born in
                    Africa,
And not all free Africans
                    Are free.
Those who want to join us
                    Join us,
But caverns such as these
                    Confuse one. Try
to find them on your
                    Own, my good
                    Fellow.
Can you tell one grain of
                    Wild rice from

                    The other?
He was born in Minas and you, in
                    Mina,
But Africans are Africans, and
not all Africans are
                    Free.
The sovas, the tribal
                    Chiefs, sold

Him,
And Senhor Negreiros, the
Portuguese
Sailor, sold
You,
But Africans are Africans and
not all Africans are
Free.
He was traded for tobacco
And English
Brandy,
And you for gold and
Contraband, but
Africans are Africans and not
all Africans are
Free.
They claim that he's docile and
you're a devil to
Enslave,
But Africans are Africans, and not
even free Africans
Are free.

There is much to do here,
Anninho.

Much to repair. Much
to build. Much to
cultivate. Much to
mine.

Join us if you want to.
Make this your New Palmares. Though
this man-of-many-
                    Names
Prefers to call these
                    Caverns no
                    Name.
Eh, my good fellows and
good woman.
Eat up.
A chicken's still a chicken, but a
man's a man,
And a woman's who she wants to be.
We are not all Africans
                    Here, though, there
are a few Mundurucus and Tupi
Indians
Who know their interest is
                    With us,
But keep to their own
                    Customs.
We learn their languages and
                    They learn
                    Ours.
We do not try to Africanize
                    Them,
Nor do they try to Indianize us.

But culture is culture.
We enrich and civilize each

Other.
There are no Romans here only
legitimate Africans and their
Legitimate
Allies,
Men and women who want to be
Who they are.
Some must be taught to be
Themselves,
But rebels are rebels.
From Mina to Palmares. Join us
if you want to, Palmaristas old
and new.

Today we coronate a king, but we
consider ourselves a
Communion of
People
Not a kingdom. . . . *The Congo*
For the
Congolese . . .
Sometimes I hear voices, eh; the old
curandero to whom I
Was apprentice
Says I have the prophet's gift
And hear future voices. . . .
The Congo for the
Congolese . . .
Today we coronate a king.

But we are less kingdom than
                    Communion.
Future voices?
Why, I hear voices from the past
Just as well and just as
                    Loud. . . .
90,000 reis for the choicest
                    Young females, eh
60,000 reis for the third-
                    Rate girls . . . We
want slavery no more we want
prisons no more
We want oppressions no more we want
freedom forever. . . .
I helped build Fort Jesus. . . . I was
in the revolution in
                    Minas
                    Gerais . . .
The Congo for the
                    Congolese . . .
Africa for the Africans!
Independence is our first
                    Objective. . . .
          And their first objection,
                    Eh?
Drink up, the best chocolate
                    In all Brazil.
Call me Cacao,
Welcome to the Cacao

Conference. . . .
There are two roads to

       African
      Revolution,
Dois Caminhas de revolução
     Africana. . . .
No free people can forget
      That Portugal,
The first Europeans . . .
Africa, the land of gold!

Tell me more, Cabinda, about
     Almeyda . . . the
     Soldier . . .

I saw a soldier, sword
     Raised, and
     Almeyda
On the riverbank, and then I
     Was grabbed
     From behind
By one of the black
     Regiment, one of
     the black
     Regiment
Fighting with the
     Portuguese, I
     Thought it was,
And then discovered it was

                One of
                Ovimbundo's
                Regiment
Who brought me to refuge
                Here.

Ovimbundo, why that's my
                Name too.
Ovimbundo.
But drink up, good fellows
                And good
                Woman.
The best chocolate in all
                Brazil.

II.

In these caverns, Almeyda, are the
waters that heal and a man-of-
many-names who claims
That you are safe
With the wise woman Zibatra, an old
friend of his and
          Prophetess.
Wise men and women know each
          Other,
As if they were drops of the
          Same water.
These leaves I chew and
dream of you
Or see you in waking.
You oil me with healing oil. The
man-of-many-names says that these
wounds are
          Not deep,
Shoulder wounds,
Almeyda,
And that I've come here not
          For the wounds but
for the spirit's

Healing.
Zibatra, who is this
                    Zibatra?
A wise woman, he says, an old
acquaintance, though they've
never met.

But wise men and women know
each other,
As if they were
Seeds from the same pod. Are
you somewhere in
                    Alagoas?
Are you hidden in the
                    Forest?
But you oil me with healing oil.
Do I dream?
I do not dream; I look
Upon you with favor,
Com bons olhos.
Here, to talk of love is
                    Improper, to
kiss is impropriety. We are
Africans, says
                    Ovimbundo.
And war and love don't mix. But I
must call you Amante
                    Anyhow.
Almeyda, Amante. Is this
                    Treachery?

The man-of-many-names is
scandalized by kisses.
Only Europeans caress with
                    Kisses.
In this New World,
You oil me with healing oil, and
kiss the wounds on my
                    Shoulders.
But they are not deep

                    Wounds,
Almeyda.

Do you hear the congadas? We
coronate a king.
But here we are all kings and
all servants too.
I do not make spears as in
                    Palmares,
Or make the poison to tip
                    Them with, though
there are others who
                    Make spears
                    And
Repair muskets.
In dreams, I return to
                    Alagoas
To search for you.
But Ovimbundo, our leader
                    Here,

Says that for now,
It is best we both stay
                    Hidden
For Jorge Velho's regiment
                    Of petitioners is
still scattered, hunting
                    Us, the
                    Palmaristas,
And searching the Barriga
                    Range.
The war is not ended. And
so I keep to this
                    Stronghold,

For it is best not to even
inadvertently lead the enemy
here.
So keep to your stronghold,
                    Almeyda.
They are still searching for us, even
along the frontier.
I dream you have been
                    Captured, and
Angola and Cabinda,
Palmaristas who have also
                    Been
Given refuge here
Confirm the wisdom of
this wise man and so I
Keep to this stronghold. It

would be rash, he says,
To seek you now, Amante, so keep
to your stronghold, and I'll keep to
mine.
Am I drugged?
There was a time I'd not have
listened even to King
                Zumbi
If he gave me such an order. I'd have
searched every
                Polegada
Of the Barriga range. Am I
not a free man?
Eu não sou um homem livre?
But by now, he says, they
know that I'm a

                Palmarista
                Too.
But by now, he says,
The petitioners have revoked
                My free
                Papers.
Using freedom, they say, to
facilitate conspirators
                Against the
                King!
And is not the king a
                Conspirator
                Against us?

Would not the king trade
Anyone of us
For a keg of English brandy?

Ovimbundo prophesies a time of no
slave traders
No slave peddlers, no
slave merchants, bartering
us for Sugar
Tobacco
Brandy
Flour
Manioc
Rum
Hides
Fish
Lumber
Gold
Leather

Dried meat
Silk
Imported carpets
Pepper
Firearms
And when we Africans
Build our own cities
Not hidden in some forest or the
Barriga range
But cities in the open even

along the frontier from
Bahia to Rio from
Pernambuco to
                    Jigonhonha from
Piaui to Maranhao from Para to
Rio Grande from Minas Gerais
to
                    Sergipe.
But between now and then,
                    Almeyda,
More slave agents
And more Captain Velhos than we
can count on all our
                    Fists.
O quilombo dos Palmares.
And not just the chalked
                    Faces,
Even pretos.
If color's not contagious, then
slavery is.
Do I dare tell you of
King Adarunga?
But the collaborators and

                    The
                    Conspirators
Always have the same faces. Here, I
do not plan war
                    Stratagems. In
Palmares, I knew King

Zumbi,
But here I do not know the
King.
Perhaps they think it's
easier not to have
Traitors,
If everyone thinks that
Everyone's the
King,
So when they coronate the King,
They coronate us all!
Ovimbundo
And Bacongo and
Quimbundo, Pedro
And Nascimiento
And Honorio,
Mandinga,
And Ioio, and
Xingar.
Here, I do not make spears or
repair firearms,
I grow yams, and
santonica,
And Indian pepper, and
agapanthus.

(Should I dare call it
The African love-flower?) And
I tend the king's
Horses.

Horses are better than
            Spears,
Says Ovimbundo. Better
than firearms. Though I
don't know who the king
is,
Or what the horses are for.

You are rubbing me with
            Healing oils,
            Almeyda,
And I am planting
            Agapanthus.
And we are in that New
            Brazil
Building our own city, our
own free city.

III.

Rebel?
You call Ioio rebel?
Me?
I am scribe, me. Free by
Benedito. Free by rebel-
monk
Who bought Ioio freedom. I am
scribe, me.
I know secret language, me. What
secret language, you
                    Ask?
Mende, man.
Kpele.
Bamum.
Calabar.
I know Old World secret
language, man, real African
language. Old African
language.
And I write them down like so.
But speaking, I speak broken
                    Portuguese.
And what I say, what say I? I

listen, me.
And what say you, what say you?
Tell me your tale, man. I
listen to

Men tale and women tale, eh,
                    Senhores and
                    Mulheres,
They always tell me Palmares story
And Zumbi story.
And Ganga Zumba tale. What
tale you tell me?
I am Ioio.
I am scribe, me.
I speak broken Portuguese, yes,
But I know secret language, as if I
born to write them.
You is fool, Ioio, Portuguese
master he say. And I write secret
language with a tamarind stick
Till the stick broke. Trying
to outsmart the
                    Master, eh?
But the master,
He always well-guarded by
                    Soldiers.
He hire he own soldiers. When the
new slaves come, the new soldiers
come.
Tell me your tale, man. Your

name?
Anninho, eh?
I don't call you liar.
Don't call me liar.
I hear that name.

I hear them other say your
                    Name.
That your true name?
Free one he come among us,
                    They say.
Free one, he come fight with
                    Us, they say.
Free African, he on
                    Horseback.
Free one, he
Jeopardize he own freedom. Fight
with Palmaristas,
                    Fight with us.
They say your name and they
                    Say the mulher
                    Name.
They say them name:
Anninho and Almeyda. They
say them name. Eh, I speak
broken
                    Portuguese,
                    Me.
Don't mean I don't
                    Understand what

you say, man.
You want know my story? I am
Ioio,
Born in Mina, traded for
tobacco, and then it's on
to Port of Bahia, eh, it's
on to Port of

          Pernambuco, it's
on to Port of Rio,
But they don't know what I
         Am, eh,
Ioruba or
Ewe,
Hausa or
Ashanti,
Bantu or
Mandinga,
Or Sudanese.
They don't know who Ioio. Ioio
the ordinary little
         Negrito,
Traded for tobacco, he,
Chewing on a tamarind stick.
Tobacco, it make me sneeze. No
Ethiopian prince, me,
But they catch me in tribe
         War, make
slavery, shrimp they call
me,
Monkey in the tamarind tree, him

one little negro, 60,000
                    Reis, you
                    Joke,
Trade him for tobacco and
                    Sweet brandy,
Master, him see me
                    Scribbling
                    Secret

                    Language, he
say, Ioio, you most
                    Devious little
                    Fool,
Ioio, you most dubious
                    Little fool.
Him give me lashings.
Rebel-monk, that Benedito, him
see the lashings.
Him a one big man, that is
                    The truth.
I think him there lash me
                    More.
Him buy me with gold
                    Shavings,
Make Ioio free.
And now I here in these
                    Cavern, and
now I write down
                    Everyone story in
these secret language. You know

these secret
                    Writing, you?
Eh, who you to know these
                    Secret
                    Writing?
Eh, who you to make good
                    Sense of
these imbroglio? Wise
man he say such one as
you
He come here these cavern make
good sense of these

Imbroglio
I am Ioio, me.
I speak pidgin Portuguee. Tell
me your tale, Senhor.
I know already *who* you are.

IV.

I am Anninho
From Minas
Born to a free man born to
a free woman
Gold and diamond washers in a
mining town.

But I see that you know that
tale already. Anyhow, your
leader,
              Ovimbundo,
And I have much in common, except
that I have just one
              Name,
Anninho,
And he has many; except that
he has many
              Wives,
And I have just one:
Almeyda.
They have told you her name? Eh, I'm
no storyteller, me.
I'm Anninho from Minas. Free

man and warrior and husband of
Almeyda,

Almeyda who knows the stars
                By their first
                Names.

But first stories first.

Zumbi, when I first came to
                Palmares,
                Distrusted me.
A spy for the Portuguese, he
                Swore.
Why would a man with free
                Papers want to
fight alongside
                Fugitives?
Why would a man with free
                Papers
Who could settle anywhere from
Bahia to Fort Jesus choose to settle
with
                Quilombistas.
But Palmares has its own
                Spies,
And the spies for King Zumbi found
me honorable,
And as I could travel to and fro
From Bahia to Fort Jesus, they

found me of great
                    Utility
They found me of great use. And
          Zumbi—the great king of
                    Palmares—
Once called me his own
                    Shield
For it shines like a mirror. That is
to say, that he could

                    See himself in
          Me.
Or me in himself. But
I'm no Zumbi. I'm
Anninho
From Minas, the mining town.

If freedom start anywhere, say
Ovimbundo.
It start in Minas.
You own your own gold mine, you?
          Or diamonds, you own
                    Diamonds?

No, my father supervises the
washings.

Hey, hey, tell me more.
Ovimbundo, he say,
If revolution start anywhere it start

in Minas.
I want no more slavey me. Tell
me more of yourself. You no
Zumbi, eh.

I'm no Zumbi. I
am Anninho,
From Minas.
Free man and warrior, and
lover of Almeyda. See how
she oils me, see how I shine!

Almeyda, who knows the stars
                    By their first
                    Names.
The birds must think that
                    She's the
                    Moon.
She's the color of the dark,
                    Golden yam.
The birds must think that
                    She's the
                    Moon.
She's a labyrinth of kisses.

Almeyda, with prominent
                    Cheekbones, her
eyes are antimony. See how
she's shining.

The most ancient birds must
                    Think that
                    She's the moon.
She's a labyrinth of kisses.

Almeyda, who knows the birds
                    By their first
                    Names.
The stars must think that
                    She's the
                    Moon.
She's the color of the dark,
                    Golden yam.
The stars must think that
                    She's the

                    Moon.
She's a labyrinth of kisses.

Should not some women see
                    Themselves in a
                    kiss
Like it was a shield?
Almeyda,
This is a New World song, I am
painting my woman
                    Golden, see
how she's shining.

She's the color of the dark,
                    Golden yam. Her
eyes are antimony, warrior and
lover, Almeyda, Tell me who's
your love?
You are, Anninho. But here's
                    Your spear and
                    Shield.
Here is your spear and
                    Shield?
Eyes of almond,
And the ecstasy of the moon.

Listen, mulheres,
How he sings her praises, when
it is the praises of
                    Palmares
He should sing.
Listen, mulheres,
How he sings her praises,

When it is the praises of
                    King Zumbi
He should sing.
Listen, mulheres,
How he sings her praises, when
it is the praises of
                    Our own
                    Ovimbundo
He should sing.

Listen, mulheres,
How he sings her praises. We
can't offend propriety,
                    Good Sir,
With kisses.
We can't afford to see
                    Ourselves in
                    Kisses,
Only in shields, shining.
The armor of the Portuguese,
                    Doesn't it
                    Make them
                    Shine!
We need knives to carve this
                    Manioc bread.
We're the wives of
                    Guerreiro, us. From
Sofala to Calcutta, New Africans,
who are you? Almeyda, of the
prominent
                    Cheekbones
And the frizzy hair
Is oiling him with kisses, is
shining him with kisses.

The Portuguese—it is their
                    Armor that
                    Makes them
                    Shine!
We need knives to carve this
                    Manioc bread.

Listen, mulheres, women of
cinnamon,
Here you will find the rumor
                    Of volcanoes
With frizzy hair.
He should sing a savage song
                    In a savage
                    Country,
Not a love song,
But Almeyda's a labyrinth of
                    Kisses, girls.

She is glowing, this
                    Almeyda,
Call her Almeyda.
She's not just any woman, eh?
We have the same fine
                    Qualities.
The same physique. The
same spirit.
But is this an age of praise
                    Songs, women?

          Tell us of the battle with
          Those devil

                    Portuguese,
Anninho.
The shields and blood. The
knives and blood. The muskets

and blood. The spears and
blood.
Tell us of the battle with
> *Those devil*
> *Portuguese,*
Anninho.
Tell us of what you vowed
> *And swore.*
Here, we are well-organized and
proud to be Africans, and think for
ourselves.
We are a nation. Bad
slaves all.
But bad slaves make good
> *Free men,*
And good free women.
Ovimbundo says that freedom is the
great cause of this
> *Century.*
The Portuguese devils are the
same anywhere in this
> *World. It*
is no mistake that
Africans are Africans.

We are the wives of
> *Guerreiro, the*
> *African.*
New Africans, who are you?

This is a New World song I
      Sing.

Old World or New,
We need knives to cut this
      Manioc bread.
New Africans, who are you?

I am a horse and she's the
      Mountain.
I'm a dolphin and she's the
      Sea.
I'm a cat and she's the
      Tamarind tree.

But she's water and you're
      The fountain.
We need knives, Sir, to cut
      This manioc
      Bread
Not kisses.
Or do you think she's
      Madeira wine?
Kisses?
You must think you're the
      Viceroy of
      Bahia.
A nobleman's a nobleman.
Hush, Curiboca. He must

Think he's the
Viceroy of Bahia.

Why, we need knives to cut
            This manioc
            Bread.

        Hush, mulheres, ripe as
        Yams.

Ovimbundo, our defender,
            Listen how
He praises a woman
Hear how he praises a woman, while
we're surrounded by
            Enemies.
Portuguese soldiers
            Everywhere,
While this gentleman-soldier sings the
praises of a
            Woman.
Should we call him knight or
            Knave?
We've told him we need
            Knives,
            Senhor,
To cut his manioc bread.
            Knives, not
            Kisses.
Ovimbundo . . .

Benedito, I am Benedito, and
Benedito's me.
We have much in common,
                    Anninho,
Except that I have many

                    Wives—
You see and hear them—And
you have one; except that I have
many
                    Names and
you are merely Anninho,
                    From
Minas, the mining town. The town
of revolutions, but that's another
story. And first stories first, eh.

I have returned from the
                    Slave traders'
                    Warehouse.
A number of the captured
                    Palmarista
                    Women
Were sold to that devil
                    Corricao.
No, Almeyda's not among
                    Them.
That devil takes his lessons
                    From me, eh?
He refuses to call me

Benedito,
Always calls
Me Negrao.
Let me take off my monk's
Robe.
I've purchased some of those
Who were
Captured

And traded provision for
Others.
We need knives to cut this
Manioc bread.
Hush, mulheres, wild as
Yams.
That devil takes his lessons
From me,
As I was saying, but one
Nation's
Marriage
Customs
Are another's decadence. One
nation's virtue is
Another's
Vice.
He picks our best women, the
women of first quality,
And the pretty
Girls
For his harem. Our

Tenderest
Women and
Robust ones
Too.
And mulattoes who chalk
Their faces!
But gold will buy anyone of
Them
To appease that devil's
Extravagant
Tastes
And his extravagant

Personality.

Bring chocolate for Anninho
And Indian tea for
me.
All wealth comes from the
Slave trade.
Imported silks, from the
Slave trade.
Gold goblets, from the slave
Trade.
Oriental silks, from the
Slave trade.
Tapestries and diamonds,
From the slave
Trade.
All wealth comes from the

Slave trade.
Mansions and palaces, from
                    The slave
                    Trade.
Every luxury comes from the
                    Slave trade.
(And every lust too.)
Eh, I have come from that
                    Devil slave
                    Trader,
But his extravagant
                    Personality
Makes even the governor
                    Wink, for
even the governor comes there to
quench his

                    passion,
Or to spice it up, eh.
Soldiers and sailors, peddlers and
businessmen, exiles and viceroys,
Ironworkers and soap
                    merchants
All come to quench their
                    Passion,
Or to spice it up, eh.
And there's one there he
                    Swears is
the daughter of the King
                    Of Dahomey.

The King of Dahomey's
                    Daughter?
I know a king's daughter
                    When I see
                    One.
He won't take gold for her
                    Or ivory
                    Either.
I know a king's daughter
                    When I see
                    One.
(All our mulheres are king's
                    Daughters
Though they're sold for
                    brandy!)

Yes, we need knives,
                    Mulheres
To cut this manioc bread,

And war horses too.
I've seen your Almeyda, by
                    The way,
No, not at the horse
                    Traders, I've
                    Told you.
But as seers see.
She knows the stars by their
                    First names,
                    Eh?

And the little birds too,
                    Your amante?
Why, I've seen her at the
                    River doing
                    Laundry,
Like an ordinary woman, which
means she's safe, as
                    I've told you,
But when she squatted the
                    Moon squatted,
And when she rose the moon
                    Rose up.
Who is this woman who
                    Carries the
                    Moon on her
                    Head?
I heard her sing your
                    Praises, by
                    The way.
She's glowing such a glow that
makes you think that
                    You're the
                    Sun, eh?

She's safe, as I've said.
But needs healing and that's
                    Zibatra's job.
Wise women seek out wise
                    Women.
As for the Portuguese

Soldiers,
They still roam about.
(They laughed at my monk's
                Robes,
But everyone knows Benedito,
                The monkish
                monk.)
They still roam about. As I
was saying,
So don't think the war is
                Ended,
And there are plenty reis
                For your head,
                Good man,
As any other fugitive, and
                More,
Free man from Minas or not, I'd
advise you again
Keep to this stronghold, praise any
woman you want
                to.
                But, yes, we need knives,
                mulheres,
To cut this manioc bread, and
war horses too.

V.

Almeyda,
Here we breed fine horses this
boy and I.
(The boy jokingly calls them
          Elephants
Because of their strength
          And endurance; and
once I dreamt that they
          Were indeed
          Elephants not
Horses;
Elephants of war all ridden
          By warriors—
Tiger-men and tiger-women.) But here
we breed horses, while I weigh the
          Advantages
And disadvantages of staying in this
quilombo already
          Formed or
striking out anew for the
          New Palmares, the
one we promised.

(The wise man speaks of it as if it
were already
                    built.)
I have become a quieter more
                    Reflective man
Than among the Palmaristas,

Though I work as vigorously
                    Here.
These are indeed fine horses of good
breeding
And taming them is easy
As if they tamed themselves. (Some
we keep wild on
                    Purpose; it
is not good for war
                    Horses to be
                    Too tame.
But know when to tame
                    Themselves,
                    eh?)
It is still a crime in this
                    Brazil
For black men and women to
                    Be caught on
                    Horseback,
And to possess so many
                    Horses, but,
Says Ovimbundo, our leader, the
superiority of the

Portuguese in
War
Is built on horseback.

I dream of you, Almeyda, and
of all the New
Palmaristas,
On horseback, led by King Zumbi. And not
in war, but riding
Freely the

Barriga range, as
free men and women.
The Portuguese Captain Velho
And his men
And all their allies
Are somewhere no doubt
Boasting and praising
Themselves
For their strategies of war ("Just war"
they call it)
For building their wall
Against our
Palmares wall
And in climbing their wall
Climbing ours.
Let them boast and praise
Themselves.
The war is not ended.

Shall I tell you
Of the New Palmares
We have vowed and sworn to
            Form?
        Those of us who escaped the
            First battle?

Almeyda, the war has not
            Ended. But
here in these caverns are the
African waters that
            heal.

                    —*Anninho, 1695*

SONG FOR ANNINHO

1.

The trees are tall here.
The men are tall.
The men are the color
of the black bark.
But men are not trees.
Sap is not blood.
Bark is not the flesh of men.
I do not believe the trees
can hear me singing.
I touch them.
Some vibrations of voice,
perhaps, my tenderness.
I kiss his mouth.
"What is it, Almeyda?"
"This is a good place,
because it is like the place
we lived before;
like our own country."

You rub my body with oil,
and heal the scars.
"Anninho was kind to me, Zibatra."

"Why wouldn't he be kind?"
"I don't know,
but he was so kind to me, my friend,
and you must tell me,
if you can truly see into time
and transformations of place."
"Why wouldn't he be?" asks Zibatra.
"You gave him what he wanted.
He got between your knees, didn't he?
Why wouldn't he be kind?"
"Ah. More than that," I say.
"What can I tell you?
It's like he took hold of me
and shaped me.
How can I tell you anything
of what I feel?"
"I can hear better than most,"
she replies.
"I can hear beyond ears."

"When Anninho and I were talking,
we saw a dead frog, the
pattern of a dead frog,
because the earth had almost
absorbed it."
"What?"
"When we were talking there
was this dead frog," I said,
"but it was no longer a frog,
it was becoming earth;

it would soon be earth.
But it still had the smell
of a frog, and something else,
something the flies and time
had brought.
I stopped the breath from
coming in my nostrils.
And then when we got past it,
I took in breath again.
It was becoming earth, don't you see?"

"Anninho?"
"Woman."

I lie on my back,
somewhere on a mountain,
my body stretching as long
as your spirit, Anninho.
A magic woman is creating
visions and voices and possibilities.

I wanted my body to become
one with the earth,
to become the earth.
And I saw it do so, Anninho,
the earth, the earth was me.
The flesh of the earth was my flesh.

Zibatra, the wizard woman—no witch—
leans forward and speaks to me,

and it seems that you touch
my forehead, Anninho.
She speaks in tongues.
anii ennana khety inini
merikere ibihe kenikhesait
iudenet ipuiwer
And there is no translation for it.
"Do you have a man?" she asks
in Portuguese and Tupi.
"Yes, Anninho. You know it."
"That is right. A woman like you
should have a man. A woman
such as this one should have
such a man as that one."
"Where is he? The battle of Palmares
ended, we escaped; Portuguese soldiers
caught us at the river.
My memory does not go beyond that.
Did you not see Anninho
when you found me?"
"No. Only the globes of your breasts
floating in the river.
I wrapped them decently and hid them.
The mud on the riverbank
had stopped the bleeding.
I put you in a blanket and
brought you here . . .
I cannot find him for you.
It is you who must make the discovery."

This earth is my history, Anninho,
none other than this whole earth.
We build our houses on top
of history.

Do you remember how it was
up in the mountains?
The sky is our symbol of immortality,
old stargazer.
Do you remember how it was, Anninho?
Why do you keep saying my name, woman?
Don't you feel and know why?

Zibatra, the wizard woman, is here
curing my wounds.
She is not confused by time,
and so I've asked her to find you.
But she says I am the one
to do the finding.
She's capable of transformations,
as if there were no boundaries
to the world—as if there were
no impossibilities in it.
Where's Anninho? I ask her, but she
tells me that I must seek you my own self
Sometimes she lets me hear your voice—
see the black eyes I remember.
I must seek you my own self
When I am whole again,

I must go on the long journey for you.
I must make the discovery my own self
cannot find him for you, she tells me; it
is not my acts or imagination
that must find him.
She tells me stories of gods and heroes,
and claims my fever and delirium.
I struggle through memory,
wondering if when I find you,
I'll please you—
the blood of the whole continent
running in my veins.

I am on the road again walking.
Bamboo bruises my knees.
I lift my skirt to walk through a stream.
I take off my shoes and tuck my skirt in.
There is a bird in that branch.
"Look."
"What?"
"Did you see it?"
"What?"
"That's all right, if you didn't see it."
"I said what, woman."
"Nothing."
"Woman."
(Is it I or Zibatra who reverses time?
Are we really together?)
You didn't see it, so it's all right.
A lovely bird though, so full of color.

You look at me with admiring eyes;
I look at you so.
Zibatra rubs the back of my neck,
rubs my shoulders, and my empty bosom.
She talks of the struggles between
desire and fear.

"What is your relationship to the universe,
and to me?"
She gives me fruit dipped in honey.
She rubs my body in oil.
The mosquitoes are getting blood.

"I like to see a woman
who passionately loves her husband,"
she says,
and then sings *wallada aie wallada aie*,
as if I could interpret her tongues.
"I am Zibatra," she tells me,
"a mystic and biblical scholar.
I'm an enchantress and a mixer of herbs.
I drunk from the vine before the vine
was invented.
What is my relationship to the universe,
or to you?
I cannot find Anninho for you,
though sometimes I agree to
phantom lovers' visits.
But you, you must go

on the long journey for him
yourself—through memory and the world.
You must mend the universe together . . .
You were born in Recife in 1669, or
thereabouts . . .
Your name is Almeyda and you're a Catholic . . .
Your greatest desire is to be a good woman . . .
Your grandmother fought in wars
against the Dutch, then the Portuguese . . .
some mystical connections . . .
You like fish and wild honey,
to hide in your shell—
OK, little turtle,
OK, little Jaboti, come out!
I like to see a woman passionately
loving her husband.
I'm an enchanter.
I like adornments and amusements sometimes,
other times I've got no humor,
I'm *desapego*;
I live like a saint;
I know places where the visible
and the invisible meet,
where the human and the divine come together.
I have seen what an ordinary human woman
does not see and know.
I have seen with a third eye,
and a fourth one, and yet another.
I have spoken in tongues, and beyond language.
Did Anninho give you that sacred jewelry,

that amulet?"

"Yes."

"Mohammedan inscriptions. A special touch,
an embrace, a kiss?

'God is just.

I confess there is no God but God.'

'Dignity is a prized possession.'

'I have a preoccupation with eternity.'

'I will protect you.'

'I am spiritual material.'

And your own rosaries from palm nuts.

I'll cure you, but you must find him
on your own . . .

Well, you'll see him in another time and place . . .

I was there when the names were given
and taken away . . . *wallada, wallada, aie, aie* . . .

Bear with me and forgive the way I am speaking . . .

This plant is Ipecacuanha that I rub on you . . .
a fast cure; and its odor brings back memory
and replenishes desire . . .

His eyes are as black as ebony,
and he has a high, heroic forehead,
a prominent nose, full lips and good character . . .
a respectable, intelligent fellow, a Muslim . . .
spiritually complicated . . .

They call him a dangerous fellow, a rebel . . .
obedient to God in the manner of our
Master Mohammed . . .
knows how to read and write anything . . .

Ah, look at all the things that lie

beyond one's choice and decision . . .
And the woman—lovely—round shoulders—
graceful—hair anointed with flowers—
a wedding—yours? . . . Do you know
Velho, that wicked, ridiculous man?
That ignorant, fanatic, miserable devil?
Do not permit me to judge.
But do you know Jorge Velho?"
"He led the expedition against us."
"You'll gather together again . . .
a New Palmares . . .
but you'll have to do the
climbing yourself.
I can't take you there."

This is a good place,
except for the mosquitoes.
I saw the frog again, Anninho.
Another one.
It was not so perfect as the one before.
It had not gotten as close to the earth.
Not so perfectly becoming earth.
It was still more flesh than earth.
And the flies, Anninho.
The flies were unbearable.

Do you remember the stairway you showed me?
The one made out of rock
and you said that no man had formed it.
That it has formed up from the earth

by God and no man.
It ran up the side of the cliffs.
You took my arm.
You called me your woman.

The mosquitoes are getting blood.

I dreamed that you had a plate,
a tin plate on your knees
and I fed you.
You cleaned off all the meat
and left the small bones.
A small thing we were eating.
A squirrel.
A sparrow.
Why am I like this?
Why can't my memory be whole?
I bite my own toenails to keep them
from curling under;
translate the past into a
lover's language.

We entered the river.
We bathed in it.
I was afraid someone would come.
I was afraid
they would come,
but you said no they would not come,
they would not find us.
It was safe.

The water was clear.
The smell of caneleira,
of cinnamon trees.

Zibatra mixes spiderwebs in water.
Ianayna, Inae, Aioka-Maria.

My grandmother's fingers are
thin and long.
She said how her skirt came to her ankles
and she would tuck her skirt
into her drawers,
to make it shorter
when it needed to be shorter,
and long when she needed the length.
We were in the cane field
and she told me how she had run
because she did not want the
white men to see her,
but they had seen her anyway,
they had seen her eyes,
and the Dutchman had purchased her;
his flying woman.

I cross my hands over breasts
that are no longer there.
You put your hands in my hair.
Zibatra is out gathering turtle eggs
to make a new oil for me.
She comes back with some holy chant

and a new tale of adventure
and inner being:
aata aie, aata aie.

A Dutch mapmaker
at the beginning of the century.
A land of deep forests,
oil-giving trees.
I am the granddaughter of an African.
This is my land.
I take palm oil and rub it on my hair and body.
This is my place. My part of the world.
The landscape and tenderness,
the wars too and despair,
the possibilities of some whole living.
A new perception.

"What do you see now, Almeyda?"
asks the wizard woman.
"My grandmother walking,
her skirt tucked in,
the way I walk now.
She takes a stick from the side
of the road or footpath
and uses it to walk some,
and then throws it away.
Her skirt tucked in."

That part of the world is greener
than this one.

I am the granddaughter of an African.

I lie on my back,
put my hands over my breasts.
"I thought my breasts were gone.
The soldier."
"You can still imagine them,
can't you? Can't I keep you
with your imagination?"
All right. Breasts then.
Anninho touches them.
"It hurts, Anninho."
"Be still."
"My shoulder still hurts,
Anninho, my shoulder is hurting.
I cry out to you.
My shoulder.
I cry out to you."
"There are no other people here.

The forests are empty.
We are the only two women
on this mountain," says the healer,
gathering together herbs.
"Were you afraid to speak to me, Anninho?"
"What do you mean, woman?"
"I felt Anninho near me, I heard his voice.
I turned around and he would not speak to me."
I taste an onion.

I feel palm oil on my hand.
"What is it you wish to say to him?"
"There are so many things I want to say.
I want to tell him it was as easy
to be with him as it was to eat food
or drink water.
I want to tell him it was not him
but the road that we were traveling
that was hard.
I want to say his name over and over again."

"I want to say the name of the woman
with the eyes that made me turn from
where I had been going.
I want to say the name of that woman
over and over again."

"Did you hear him?"
He stands there.
Don't you see him watching me,
and then when he has finished watching,
he turns and walks away without looking back?
"Anninho, why are you watching me?
Don't look at me like that.
Or say something. Speak to me."
"He doesn't have anything to say."
"Nothing?"
"No."
And what if I say his name over and over?

The eyes of the man who made me turn
from the way I had been going.
Together we made a whole way.

My tongue runs into his mouth
till I think he will swallow it.

"How did you find me, Anninho?"
"Your blood left a path on the stones.
I followed the path of your blood."
He handed me sandals and he knelt down
and strapped them to my feet.
"Ask me to, Anninho."
Then in that time and that small place
we had made for each other,
even our souls were beating one
with the other.
"Does it hurt?"
"Yes, but go on. Sometimes it is the hurt
that heals."
I want to make a place on the earth,
a place where some part of us can grow deep.
"Has it always been this way, Anninho?"
"How?"
"Between men and women."
"Yes."
I will plant my womb in the earth,
and it will grow,
and this feeling we have made between us
will grow as deep.

We walked up the stone steps
that he said no man had formed
that only God himself
had formed,
and he spread the blanket,
and we were married there.

"It hurts, Anninho."
"What, woman?"
"Something is hurting me, Anninho."
"You must know what it is."
"This part of my back,
when I bend this way.
And something else.
Something beyond that.
Something other than that."
"And you'll be whole again,"
says the healer.
"Where does it hurt?"
"Woman, hush.
Your voice is a burden now.
My name is a burden on your tongue."
"Anninho, don't. Anninho.
Don't move away from me, Anninho.
Remember that day.
You made me expose every part of me
to show you where the pain was.
When I said here and here and
here and here too,
then you believed me.

Why not now?
Was it because you had a pain yourself then?
And because then you wanted to put mine with yours,
so that they'd heal each other?"
We lay there.
We were exhausted with going from
place to place.
We had left the others,
and journeyed on our own.
Trees and shadows.
"We should go on, Anninho."
"Come here."
"But Zumbi said . . ."
"He said that there is always a last day,
when the blood of the hunted
serves as a guide for the hunters."
"Don't say that, Anninho."
"Yes, that day will come, woman.
But before that day comes,
let this happen. Now come to me."
I was a whole woman and he was a whole man then.
And then he became angry.
Something had made him angry.
I was sitting there,
the blanket wrapped around
only the lower part of my body.
Something had made him angry.
He had that moment of anger
before his great tenderness.
The trees seem greener here.

"What made you angry?"
"Nothing."
"Having to leave one place
and go to another, always?"
He doesn't answer.
"I wanted to be with you, Anninho."
"When?"
"From the beginning."

"I have seen it done to others.
There was a woman,
as tall as a tree,
as tall as if she were walking on stilts.
They cut off her breasts.
She had made them angry.
Something she had done,
or not done.
In this country,
that is one of the things
they do to the women."

"Be still, woman. Move closer to me."
"Anninho, I want to give you children."
"What?"
But it was neither the time nor the place
for such wishes, and we got up to go on.
What is it your eyes are telling me?
You won't answer.
Let your eyes speak, then.
Let my own eyes speak.

"Is this your husband?"
"Yes, this is my husband.
Anninho's his name.
We have been together every way
that the spirit, the mind and the body can be.
We have been together every way."
"Is this man, Anninho, your husband?"
"Yes."

The mosquitoes are circling and taking blood
when they want it.

"Beautiful woman."

Our eyes kept wandering to other worlds,
and when they were tired of wandering,
they set upon each other.

"I want to stay here, Anninho."
"There won't be any way
you can stay here.
When they catch us,
they'll take you back."
"The men they kill,
the women they take back."
"Yes."
"Sometimes they take the men back.
They have taken men back."
"Not often."
"Not you?"

"No."
"Then they won't take me back.
There is one way I can stay."
He looked at me hard. "No."
"Wouldn't it be better?"
"No."
"For you it would be better,
but not for me."
He says nothing.
"I'm your woman, Anninho,
I always want to be your woman.
They won't keep me your woman."
"You'll still be my woman.
Let's go this way."
He kissed me before we went.
"Did you hurt yourself?"
"No."
"You should have been looking.
You did hurt yourself."
"No."
"There's blood around your toes.
It's slippery here.
Be careful.
Why are you standing there
looking at me like that?"
"They'll find us, won't they?
How many men escaped with Zumbi?"
"Ten, I think."
"No more than ten?"
"No more. Maybe less than ten."

Anninho made a necklace of shells
for me. We found some acorns.
A necklace out of shells and
acorns and some kind of seeds.
I don't remember what kind.
What kind of shells?
I don't remember what kind.
You loved him.
Yes, I told you that.
You're a beautiful woman.
He must have loved you.
I hope not because I was beautiful.
I hope not for that reason.
Because there was something
beyond that then.
Does that make you feel better?
Yes.
Something beyond that,
what does it matter?
Because it matters.

"The trees, Anninho. Look at the trees."
But he looked beyond trees.

The palms of our hands were plates.

I picked up a stick and used it for
walking a part of the way.
I knew then, Anninho, when we were

walking, I knew there would be a time
when I would want to bring that time back,
when I would want to make this time
and that time the same one.

"Who made the earth so that his blood
and mine could not continue together?
And we had to turn our backs on each other,
and be silent.
Who made the earth that way?
You are the wise one,
tell me when I shall find him?"
"Memories continue, return together.
Spirits continue together."
"Speak in my language."
"You will be."

I want to grab hold of him again.
I want him to grab hold of me.
I want us to be gloves for each other.
What is the meaning of our wanderings
in this new world?

"Can you make it?"
"Yes."

"What are you thinking, Almeyda?"
asked the woman who did not need to
struggle with time or place.

"He is taking hold of my hands again.
The gravel is loose. He keeps
me from falling. I grab hold of his hand
and the branch of a tree."

"Can you make it?"
"Yes."
"I think the others came by this way."

We rest and I hug his knees.
He thinks it is a silly thing,
and so I sit away from him,
hugging my own knees.

When we rest, I hug my own knees.

He is standing with his back to me.
He is watching something.
There is a circle of sweat on the
back of his shirt.

*"Do you remember the day they let
the devils loose?"*
"Yes."
*"They mixed blood with water
and were sipping it like
we would sip cocoa."*

Sometimes I pretended it was not
Anninho and I escaping, but

all of us together.
We had formed a column,
the men and the women and children.

A long line,
each person behind the next.
I was walking behind Anninho;
each person was following someone.
Everyone who was strong
had a bundle on their head
or strapped to their shoulders or back.
Anninho wanted to carry mine and his, too.
But I kept mine.
And that is the way I imagined it,
one behind the other
because we had all escaped together.
But we always move from one dangerous
place to another.
Hush.
We all do.

There are places to rest.
Yes, we came to a place to rest,
didn't I say so, and Anninho
sat on a rock and I sat near him
and hugged his knees.
He thought it was a silly thing,
and so I hugged my own.
This is the way the dream went, Anninho.
I am not Anninho, I am the medicine woman,

but tell me your dream.
This is the way the dream went.
I kept making feathers for you.
No, they were not from birds.
They were woman-made.
Each piece I put there myself
I don't know what it could mean, Anninho.
There I was sitting on a blanket
you had spread for me,
my legs folded together.
The top of my body was bare,
and the blanket covered the lower part of me.
I made the feathers from nothing.
What could it mean, Anninho?
Whatever it meant, while I was
in the dream, it frightened me,
but when I awoke from it,
it gave me hope.
It was strange because
it was like I had to keep making feathers.

There was no choice in the matter.
It was something that had to be done.
It was my responsibility to do it.
I did not do it freely,
and yet our freedom depended on my
doing it. Is that understandable?
Yes.
What if the dream comes again?

Then it will come.
What if it does?
Then it will come.

"Pick up your things, woman,
we are moving."

It will come again, Anninho.
The dream and the feelings that went with it.
Hush.

I balanced my bundle on my head.

He said it was my eyes that
drew me to him. Not my voice,
because in the beginning,
I was not talking. It was
not anything else I possessed.
The other things came later.
But it was my eyes first,
and what they revealed of the soul.
Not your silence?
Maybe. I remember he said,
"This woman isn't talking."

We were together a long time
before I spoke with him easily.
How long?
A long time.

Maybe it seemed longer than it was.
Perhaps. Time has that way.
And then it seemed as if you'd
always been talking?
Yes.

This is a song I am singing, Anninho.
All of the women are singing.
I was afraid, Anninho,
and then after talking to you,
after I stood with you,
I wasn't afraid any longer.
I stood with you
and then we lay together.
It was much later
that we lay together.
I'd been with you a long time
before we lay together.
Then you strung the beads for me.
Seeds and shells.

I wanted to grow deep for you,
something more than feelings,
something of spirit,
all of my memory and yours,
dreams, and the whole time
we have spent with each other,
and beyond time;
and even our fears,
yes, made out of even our fears.

When you spoke to me, I stopped fearing.

This is the way it was, Anninho,
when I stood beside you and you
made me a necklace of seeds.
Seeds from some fruit we had eaten.
I placed one in your hands
and you placed one in mine.

When you spoke to me, I stopped fearing.

I wanted to be with you, Anninho,
but Zumbi said that only the men
could follow that path.
The women must wait, and the men
would return for us.
We waited.
The men returned.

You caught a fish and I pasted it
with oil and pepper.
There was no salt.

We were lucky.
It was more than luck.
Don't speak of luck in this world.
It was something beyond luck.

You left the bones on your plate.
I ate the head and the eyes.

You put some meat from your plate
onto mine.
I said no, you needed the strength
more than I.
But neither of us took it.
I wrapped the small piece of meat
in a torn rag.
But when we left, we forgot it.
It stayed there on the stone.

I still vision you standing there,
your legs astride.
You speared the fish.
Your feet were on two stones.

Next, we will eat meat that has
blood on it, you said,
and found a small squirrel.

I watched you put the seeds
on a string for me.
They were seeds that came from
the meat of some fruit we had eaten.
Some kind.

This is how you found me, Anninho.
My grandmother and mother were
on a sugar plantation.
My father was some black adventurer,
if you believe there were

black adventurers in the world.
At first, I was on the sugar plantation.
Then, a shoemaker wanted me.
I was sold to him.
He taught me how to mend shoes
and other articles of leather.
I worked in a room with
two men slaves.
Every day his wife would come
and stand in the door watching me.
She would stand with her breasts bared
and a baby sucking on her nipples.
She would stand there watching.
She would stand so we could barely
see her, sometimes, but she would
be standing there.
Perhaps she thought her husband
wanted me for some other reason
than mending shoes.
If he did, he never got
me past mending shoes.
Once, I sewed a piece of leather wrong
and he spanked my hand with
the heel of a shoe until it bled.
His wife was standing in the door
with a smile on her face.
The two black men were frowning.
The baby was sucking on the woman's
breasts. She just kept smiling.
It made her happy.

When I took up the leather to sew again,
my hand bled into it.
That was my situation when
the men from Palmares stole me away.
They killed no one.
They could have killed the shoemaker
and his wife and baby,
but they didn't;
they only wanted to free us.
And it was not necessary for them to kill
to free us.
If it had been necessary, they would have.
They have killed on such raids.
When it was necessary.

I pasted the fish with oil and pepper.
I oiled my hair. You watched me.
I oiled my hands and shoulders,
and then yours.

"Where are you going?"
"To the river."
"It is not safe there. Let me come."
I let him see only my breasts for
the first time and then I told him
he must turn his head.
"Anninho?"
"What?"
"Turn, now."

It was only my eyes that he kept watching
before he watched any other part of me.

"Almeyda, wake up; it's time to move."
I found my bundle.

"Anninho."
"What?"
"I saw them."
"A dream?"
"Yes, I saw soldiers in it."
"Hush. Can you make it up this way?"
"Yes."

The first time, we were traveling
with the others, and the
last time, Anninho, you and I
were traveling alone. I speak of
both times, the time of glory,
and the time of confusion.

"You should always wear your hair
like that, Almeyda. It becomes you."

I follow you. We climb until
my legs are paining, but I won't
tell you.

"The shoemaker's wife stood in the door
watching me, and then when her

husband beat my palm until blood came,
she smiled."

The mosquitoes are drawing blood.

I gather together leaves.

I remember what your eyes were saying
the first day we met.
"How do you know you weren't putting words
in my eyes?"
"Because you're here, aren't you?"

Men were always reading my grandmother's
eyes wrong. Every man that saw her
would read her eyes wrong.
They would think they saw things,
each of them would think
they saw things that weren't there.
What they wanted.
She had those possibilities for only one man.
But she had the kind of eyes that each man
saw in them what he wanted to see,
or what he must.
They were deceived.
Not by her, but by themselves.
Their own words and memories put there.
Even when she grew old,
men were still seeing things.

"How do you feel? Are you rested?"
"Yes."
"You look sad."
"Yes."
"Did I read your eyes wrong in the beginning?"
"No."
"You must have inherited your grandmother's eyes.
Anything I want I can find there."
"I love you, Anninho."
I oil my breasts and stomach.
"Now, all you have to do is salt and pepper yourself.
You look good, woman."
"What?"
"They look as if they are offering me everything."
"What?"
"Your eyes. I can tell you see me.
I could never tell that about any other woman."
"I love you."
"You should always wear your hair like that.
It becomes you."

I pull a scab. It runs blood.
You tell me I should not have done that.
It will form a new scab.
Always a new one.
And if you keep pulling it off
before it's healed, a newer one,
and yet a newer one.

"Love me. Are you still afraid of me?"
"No."
"I've got into your blood, woman?"
"Yes."

We were sitting there, Anninho,
with the others, and you
turned to me.
You said nothing, you just turned to me,
and it was then I knew.

That was the question, Almeyda,
how we could sustain our love
at a time of cruelty.
How we could keep loving
at such a time. How we could
look at each other with tenderness.
And keep it, even with everything.
It's hard to keep tenderness
when things all around you are hard.

A legacy of tenderness.

Then you've lost nothing.
You remember how to look at
each other. How to touch.
Tenderness is a deeper thing
than cruelty.

"Do you remember when I came
and sat by you?"

"Yes. You said nothing,
but it was then that I knew."

"Come and go for a walk."
"All right."

She said, You are the granddaughter
of an African, and you have
inherited a way of being.
And her eyes stayed on mine, Anninho,
until all her words and memory
and fears and the tenderness
ran through me like blood . . .
That was the moment when I became
my grandmother and she became me.
Do you know what I mean?
Yes.
Our spirits were one.
Yes.
But it was more than that.
Yes. We are never alone.
We keep everything.
Yes.

What was wrong with you that day?
What day?
You came and stood by me twice.
You didn't say one word. You just
came and stood near me.

I don't remember.
Memory is a woman.
For a woman, memory is a man.

I kept watching how small your waist was.
Thinking what it would be like to have
my arms around you. I wonder if when a
man and woman feel something between
themselves other people feel it.
They must.
Then it depends on the people.
Some men and women when they're
together you can't tell there's anything
between them. It is all their feelings.

"Get up from the ground, Almeyda."

They saw my grandmother and then one
of them said, "I see where Almeyda
gets her beauty." Even as an old woman,
even when she was an old woman, they could
still see it.

I remember things I could not see then.
Yes, that is the way.
I have heard things again that I
could not hear then.
Yes, that is the way.
She always talked about possibilities
in the world, as if she had some choice.

They say she had links with the invisible
world. I've heard her talk to the
invisible ones.
That is the way.
She said someday I would have links
with that world . . . Perhaps she meant
the things we can't see until a new time . . .
and place . . . Eh, I don't know. So much
I feared then. She told me to fear the world
I didn't know. Not that one . . . that world
of hardships and deceptions I knew already.
Eh, that was nothing. Eh, it was the
spiritual hardships that one feared.
Eh, everyone talks about "spirit"
but no one knows it. All the times
when the day's work was over, she would sit,
not moving, still, passive; but inside she
was full of activity—everything changing.
And on holidays, when others were reveling,
she'd be that way, too—very still. You only
know her from Palmares, and so you don't know
her before she took up arms against the Portuguese.
Some people only know swords they can see.
But she wielded swords then, too.
She's the one who needs to be looked at
very closely. She's the one you can't glance
at and know. Do you think she escaped
the destruction? She has escaped,
and is in some forest, and even if they
captured her and took her back, they

wouldn't know the mystic from the poet
from the clown. She'd have her games
with them . . . Why are you smiling, Anninho?
Why are you watching me so? . . . Sometimes
I feel, Anninho, that the whole world can
feel this whole thing between us . . . Do you
know why I think she survived the destruction?
Tell me.
Because she could see everyone as herself, eh,
she's somewhere detaching herself from
the world, and flowing into it.
She's probably somewhere conversing
with some Jesuit priest, exchanging viewpoints.
She always liked to converse with them.
She'd say if there were any "knowledgeable fellows"
in Pernambuco, it would be a Jesuit.
There's nothing else for a "knowledgeable fellow"
but priesthood.
The one at the first place we were
would talk to her, but others
they'd rebuff her for her "fancied dignity"—
her "hypertenence"—some new word
they made up for any African seeker,
but every time she'd hunt out the Jesuits . . .
She was a Mohammedan, too, but had to pretend
Christianity.

"Am I a woman, or the memory of a woman?"
"What do you mean?"
"I don't know what I mean."

"In the space between your eyes, I see the words
for our feelings."

"Anninho, I."

"Don't be frightened."

"I'm not . . . Were you angry with me,
Anninho?"

"When?"

"You looked as if you were angry with me."

"I wasn't."

"You had that look. You were angry."

"It wasn't for you, it was for something else."

"I want to be as necessary as your blood, Anninho,
your spirit."

He frowns.

"*That* makes you angry."

"No."

"I can see it."

"A woman should never want to be as necessary as
a man's blood, or his spirit. A woman should
never let a man mean everything to her."

"You're as necessary as my blood,
as my spirit."

"You shouldn't let any man mean that much."

I frown.

He frowns.

I kiss him.

"What were you dreaming?"

"I was dreaming of feathers I made for you."

"You didn't say they were for me.
You told me of making feathers."

"Didn't I? This time I knew who they were for.

All of the women were sitting on blankets
their men had given them. They were all
naked to the waist, making feathers.
And didn't the war end like that?
Only cliffs to be jumped from, or surrender?
If you hadn't made that hiding place . . .
Now there are more roads in your forehead.
I tried to push the dream away, Anninho.
Not the dream, but the feeling that went
with it. I could have stood the dream,
but not that feeling. I did not know what
it meant until after the thing had happened
in the world. And our brave Palmaristas,
jumping from cliffs rather than surrender.
Oh, if they could have become birds then!
Oh, had I a net! But what the god doesn't grant!
Even now I watch out for birds,
hoping it's some Palmarista!
We are blessed because we did not just survive
that, but we survived it loving.
We never stopped loving each other."

Men are always watching. Have you
noticed that? Men are always standing
watching something. I would come upon him
and there he'd be watching. I'd be
watching him and he'd be watching that
something else.
What is it?

Nothing.
Then he would look at me.

"Your arms are paining."
"No."
"I can tell they are."
"No."
"Let's stop, now."
We slept.
The ache between my shoulder blades.

"You're always watching, Anninho."
"I suppose."
"How did you come to Palmares; did
they steal you; did you escape here?"
"No. I was a free man. I was born free.
I heard of Palmares and came here by choice.
I am useful as a spy, because I pass freely.
I am also useful in trade. I've been here
since Ganga Zumba, the foolish old man,
was leader. I was here when he believed
the Portuguese's silver promises and would
have delivered us all up to them.
I was here when Zumbi killed his foolish uncle
and became leader. It is only here that there
is dignity and position.
Freedom lives in the perpetual threat of
destruction. I am free inside this world and
outside it, but the others have freedom always
in arms."

"I have freedom in arms," I say, smiling,
but he continues his talk of weapons.
Then I ask, "Why must they always try to
destroy us? Why can't they let us stay in
this place we have made for ourselves?"
He says nothing. He is watching again.
I kiss his back through his clothes.

I wouldn't have borne anything if I'd
had to bear it alone. I couldn't have
stood alone. I'm not that kind of woman
who can stand alone. But you, before I came . . .
I do when I must, he said.

They're always watching.
Every time you find a man, they're
always watching.
We watch them and they watch something else.

The forests here are thick.
Vines entangling trees.
An abundance of palm.
But there are trees in another
part of the world that are greener than these.
Greener than the Alagoas.
Greener than the Mundahu Valley.

I was born here.
I was not born free.
I am the granddaughter of an African,

and that is why I carry my head a certain way.
The women from my grandmother's village
were proud and graceful women,
even when the burdens they carried were
greater than they were.
One always carries some burden on one's head.
Even in free times, there is never a free time.
My grandmother taught me how I must walk.
My grandmother was the one who told me about
how men are always watching, and yet, whenever
I'd see her, she'd be watching. Watching
like she could see farther than the eye
could see, like she could see the unseen
even in the seen. She'd look at me like
she saw beyond me, in time and distance,
and beyond those. But you knew her in Palmares—
that incredible woman.

This is a country that doesn't allow men
to be gentle. White men or black men.
It doesn't allow them to be gentle.
It is not easy to remain tender. It is
a very hard thing. You are a giant man,
but a gentle one. She did not know of you
when she said those things. Yet when the
roughness is needed . . . You give dangers and
survive them.

Anninho watched me.

And she said it is not easy to love
at a time such as this one. It is not
easy for a man or a woman. But she did
not know of you when she said those things.
It is not difficult to love you in any time.

Anninho stood against the rock.
There was no space between himself
and the rock.
I tried to put my arm around him
but there was no space between him
and the rock. I wanted to make sure
he had not grown into the rock.

"Before I knew you, I kept thinking
you were such a strange man."
"And you don't now? I have lost my strangeness?"
"No."

It is because we were free in Palmares
that they wanted us and the land.
We did not defeat them this time,
but the land did. How many of them
perished just in hunting us?
How many were just killed by the land
and exhaustion and hunger and disease?
Let them take over the old Palmares and
we'll have our new one.
Don't you see them coming again, and always?
"Those who discover a land, Almeyda, the way

these men know how to discover land, feed other
men to the land. That is the only way they
know how to keep it, by feeding other men to it.
Feeding it men that are already there,
and bringing new men to feed it.
But the land knows nothing . . . It takes
whatever it's given."
"I believe the land knows. It could reject
what it wants to."
He said nothing. His eyes found something to
watch again.
"That it could spit the unfortunate ones up?"
he said after a while.
"Yes."
"Maybe one day it will."

A man watches and a woman watches the man watch-
ing.
What does the land do?
The land is there where it always was and
always will be, changing times.

"They'll come to the new place."
"Let me kiss you, Anninho."
"I can't even dream the things I want to dream.
Ah, there are so many things to dream of doing.
There are nights when I wish to dream
about you, Almeyda, like a man dreams
about a woman he loves and cares for,
and even that dream . . . But in the New Palmares,
we'll create our lives again."

"Let me kiss you, Anninho.
Stand away from the rock so I can put my arms
around you. Stand away. Let me see your hand.
You must have scraped it against some rock.
Is it better now?"
"I wanted to dream about you, Almeyda,
like a man dreams about a woman he loves.
I couldn't even dream about you.
Something kept pushing the dream away.
A man wants to dream about a woman like you . . ."
"Don't talk like that, Anninho.
Stand away so I can hold you."
He stands away. He has not grown into rock.
I hold him. I want him to grow into me now,
if he must grow into anything in this world.
I want us to be one whole flesh and spirit.
He holds me for just a moment and then his arms
drop away, and he picks up his bundle.
I pick up mine.
"I dreamed of you, Anninho. I dreamed that
the eyes in your face got deeper and deeper.
And you pulled me into them.
You took me in, and the deeper I went,
the deeper there was to go."
"I didn't think you would like me."
"What?"
"In the beginning, I didn't think you would like me."
I say nothing. I watch the sweat coming
out of his shirt.

We are walking. You cannot hold a man and walk,
not when each of you carries a burden.

I wanted to prove something to you, Anninho.
I wanted to prove I was a woman.
I wanted to do something for you
that would prove I was a woman.
Why would you want to prove that?
Why would a man want to prove to a woman he's a man?

There will come a time, Almeyda,
when it won't be difficult
to be tender, when it will be an easy thing.
Do you believe that, Grandmama?
Yes.

"Anninho, I thought you had grown into the rock.
I thought you had become rock."
"No."
"Or that the rock had become flesh, and grown
into you?"
"Who knows what flesh has become rock, and what
rock flesh?"
"I prefer the rock becoming flesh, and then
changing into spirit. Is that the way things
progress in the world, and outside of it?"

"Do you remember the walk you took me on?
It wasn't because we had to, like now,
but because we wanted to. Do you remember?"

"Yes."

"It was good then, wasn't it?"

He doesn't answer. He is not the kind of man

who will answer such a question.

I watch his back,

as he pushes aside branches to help me along.

"Yes, it was good," he says.

How many steps did he take before he answered?

"I wanted to say something to you,

even at the beginning, Anninho,

but I was afraid to.

I wanted to go up to you. Say something. Anything."

Come and go for a walk with me.
Where?
Then his eyes got so deep I couldn't bear it
any longer, and I went with him.

"Grandmama said there was too much hurt in the world

for a man to add his hurt to a woman, or a woman

add her hurt to a man."

"Did I hurt you, Almeyda?"

"No, that is not what I mean. I've been telling

you such things as she told me. And that was

one of them. I've been talking them as I remember."

"Have I not hurt you?"

"Once. A little thing now. Such a small thing."

"I don't remember what I did."

"You said, 'This woman only looks at a man.'"

"You dreamed it."

"No."
"You did dream it."
"No, Anninho."
"I said it was a dream."
"All right. But it hurt, dream or no dream.
And they all watched me then. You made them
all watch me. I wouldn't look at you. It made
me understand how feelings about a man . . ."
"What?"
"Nothing."
"You were going to say it."
"It was a strange time for me. I never got over
the hurt."
"Then I did hurt you."
"No. It was my feelings. It was the way I
was feeling all that time. It was the way I was feeling
that made me watch you."
"I wanted words to take the place of watching."
"Also, she said there would come a time when
the hardness wouldn't be demanded,
that the hardness would only be something
to remember but not to hold on to.
And then the hardness must be forgotten . . .
'This woman only looks at a man' was what you said . . .
She said the hardness must give way to the
tenderness. An enduring tenderness . . . I'm tired,
Anninho. My legs are paining."
"Sit here."
He rubs my legs and knees.
"What about the muscles in your own legs?

Don't they pain?"
He says nothing. He goes on rubbing my legs and knees.
"Now you'll get tired."
He says nothing.
"It's all right. I feel better now."
He goes on rubbing.
"I was scared in the beginning, Anninho.
If I were not with you."
He goes on rubbing.
He squeezes the muscles in my legs.
He squeezes my calves.
"If it were not for you.
It was as if I was going over the edge of a cliff,
and you flew down and caught me."
"Flew?"
"Yes. And scooped me up in your arms,
like a bird, like a fierce bird."
"It was you I was watching."
"What?"
"Of all the women that we'd captured
and brought there."
His eyes, among trees, got deeper.
"Before, I held to my conviction,
that this wasn't the time or the place for
a woman. The others chose women,
but I chose none. When you were brought
into the gates, even before I questioned you,
I had decided I would create time.
And what's time if one does not create it?

There is neither time nor place for us here
unless we create it."

"When you are angry, the anger takes over
your whole body, your blood, everything.
I am afraid of you then.
I keep watching your eyes,
and it's like you can't see me.
And then after the anger is over,
your look of tenderness for me.
I am the new woman, then, Anninho,
and you are the new man."
He laughs, says nothing, while I speak
of transformation through love and tenderness.
"We are different, not new," he says.
He watches me.

"What is the right time and place?
Suppose I had said, 'This isn't
the right time, Anninho'? But love
exists in spite of time and place."
His eyes, deeper, watching.
"I saw your anger, Anninho."
"I didn't mean for you to see it.
I wanted to love you without your seeing it.
But this is a place of anger and you can't
turn the anger off, even in loving.
I wanted to come to you without anger,
to soften my eyes for you."
"I wanted to pull you into me, Anninho.

I wanted to make it so that the anger would
never return, would never have to return.
Would have no need to return. I wanted to
chase it away forever. Or cook it and eat it
if that would do away with it. It was a
hideous thing, but I would have swallowed it
whole, if l thought that would do away with it.
But the time and the place wouldn't change.
And so your anger kept. Do you think a day will come
when men will forget what anger is, will have
no need for it? Do you think so in this world?
And then the day when the hardness would be over,
the ground would soften, and swallow the anger.
And the men who know how to make the ground bleed,
and how even to get blood from stones, would
forget that knowledge. They wouldn't remember
it anymore."
He doesn't answer.
"There was a woman, Anninho, who mutilated herself,
so she wouldn't have to have any man at all.
She had done it, because she didn't want
any man at all, not the black ones or the white ones.
There was something she did to herself so that
no man would go near her."
"Did she ever have a man?"
"I don't think so. I think as soon as she discovered
how they would use her, she did that horror to herself."
"Did away with her womanhood."
"She was still a woman."
"You know what I mean."

"Yes. But there was nothing about her that was not
a woman, except the thing she had done to herself.
She wore leather bracelets and necklaces of
trumpet shells. Men found no way in.
Why are you laughing? It isn't funny."
"I'm not laughing because it's funny.
That laugh had no humor in it.
Can't you tell a laugh with no humor in it?"
"Grandmama told me she knew it was not true."
"What? About a laugh with no humor in it?"
"No. She told me she knew it was not true that
there would come a time when the hardness would
be over. There would not come such a time,
never in her lifetime and not in mine and not
in the lifetimes of those that come after us."
"That's a sore prophecy."
"She said that the Portuguese who fight us here
will fight others like us, others with the same
flesh and blood and dreams, and it will be another
time and place; it will be on the other side of the
world."
"How does she know this?"
"She knows. She said the hardness would go on.
Here, and in some other time and place.
She said that cruelty was indestructible.
Men are destructible, but cruelty goes on.
She said it is only spirit that is a match
for cruelty. But flesh, ah flesh.
She put on a halo made of feathers and
told me these things. She would laugh at

the nature of people in the world.
With all its possibilities,
she'd tell me how folks would come to her
for sexual magic—
problems of sterility and impotence.
Not just the slaves, I mean.
The masters, too, except they'd send for her.
And she'd go to them with her supplies.
'With all the problems and possibilities
in the world,' she'd say. 'They'd send
for me as a macumbeiro. They only
want me for sexual cures with all the
other possibilities in the world!
Or some silly thing like making
the eyelashes grow longer, or the hair!
Ah, the world never changes.
Anything I prescribe for them, they do.
Come and climb that hill with me, Almeydita.
When I lose my powers, I'll have to
hide in the trunk of a hollow tree!'
What she meant by that, I don't know.
Do you think she's escaped and at some
new sugar farm, being sent for—
putting huge rings on her fingers
and huge earrings that make her ears
look longer, and old satin shoes
and a sheepskin wrapped around her
shoulders, because they think that's
the way a macumbeiro should dress,
and not in plain muslin like

everybody else? Eh, she's somewhere
taking care of herself. She could
escape if she wants to, knowing
the invisible world the way she does,
but she likes to play games,
and move with the times.
When we were at Palmares,
just before the final battle,
she'd come and move her hands
up and down in front of me three times
without touching me.
I didn't tell you that—
but that was some magic; to protect me;
and my protection would
carry to you . . ."

This is the wrong time for a woman.
That's what I thought you would tell me.
That I would come to you and you would
send me away saying, This is the wrong time
for a woman.
And you, Almeyda, you could have said,
This is the wrong time for a man.
Your silence and mine and then you would
say, Leave me, Anninho, for this is no
time for a man.
Go away, woman, I thought you would say,
for this is no time for a woman.

This is a time I can't even dream
of a woman, and you bring your flesh here.
Not just my flesh, my spirit, too.
But I can't even dream of a woman.
This is the wrong time for a man and a woman.
This is not the right time.

"She said it was the wrong time for a man."
"Who?"
"The woman I told you of, the one who
mutilated herself. My grandmother said
that she'd only had to come to her,
and she would have charmed the men away,
as she had charmed men to women. Ah, what
a beautiful woman. My grandmother could
have changed her without changing her."

Think about language. We will
make words out of words.
We will use the same words,
but they will be different.

"My grandmother always talked about how we
lost our language here,
but she was speaking Arabic when she
came here, so she had already
lost her original one generations before."
He smiles.
"Why are you smiling, Anninho?"
He smiles again.

They had taken the language
and she had tried to piece it
back together like a crazy quilt,
but she had forgotten the old words,
and had to put new words in the place
of the old ones.

" 'That is what saddens me, Almeyda,' she said.
'They have taken the language. I was afraid
that would happen. I feared that more
than anything when I began this journey here.'
But she did not have her original language
even when she began it."

What day is it? I lose time in this place.

This is no time for a woman,
that is what I thought you would tell me.
If you were standing in a place,
I wanted to come and stand near you,
Anninho, but I was afraid you would resent it.
I was afraid you would resent the others
knowing how I felt. I wanted to be
wherever you were, Anninho.
I wanted to come and stand near you
or sit near you when you were sitting
near the fire. Wherever I saw you,
I wanted you to find me there.
But I didn't want to burden you.
I wanted to be as inconspicuous as your blood.

Blood is conspicuous.
I thought it was the wrong time and place,
Anninho, but I wanted you to see me.
I wanted to be with you . . . You were
apart from the others. And I had a choice
between coming near you or the others.
And I went near you. And that was
when you looked at me that way.
You spoke to me, but the look on
your face, I won't forget it.
I couldn't bear it, Anninho, and
after that, I was afraid to come near you again.
I don't remember it. Yes, I remember
you were there, but how
could I have such a look for a woman who . . .
He doesn't finish it.
I wanted to be with you, Anninho,
to stay with you, but when a man gives
a woman that look.
I didn't know I had it.
My sandals have grown thin.
They've been with me as long as I've
been with you.
It seems longer than it has been.
And if we hadn't had such
a long journey, they would still be whole.
Why do we do these things to each other, Anninho?
What things?
The things we do. Because afterwards
I found out you wanted

to be with me as much as I wanted
to be with you. And we stayed
away from each other, and then finally
you came for me. "Go for a walk with me."
My grandmother would tell of a man and a woman
who failed to speak words that should have
been spoken. The words were kept away
so long that the men and the women
forgot how to use them, and their mouths
took another shape so that they could
not use them. They could use
other words, but not those words.
They remembered the words,
but could not use them.
And those words became the
words that men and women do not
say to each other. The words
ceased to be words and became tenderness.

"Anninho."
"What?"
"I needed to speak your name."

"Your sandals are wearing thin."
"That's what I told you."
"I will have to make you new ones
from the bark of trees."
"Anninho, don't pick at the scab
on the back of your hand,
it will only make it worse."

He doesn't heed me.
He picks it off and the skin
is raw underneath.

I keep repeating myself, Almeyda.
But the repetition is necessary.
What I tell you must stay.
Yes, Grandmama.
It must become a ritual for living.
Do you hear me?
Yes.
And the words brought the hardness
into her face, and the
hardness was again replaced by tenderness.
This is not an easy thing, this life,
but this you know already without the telling.
Yes.
And she sat me to listen to the long truths.
I was young then, but I still remember them.
She had them. I swear it. Truths for a woman
to know.
Are there different truths
for a man?
He laughs.

"The skin is raw underneath, Anninho,
don't touch it. Now
it is exposed to bang against rocks
or scrape against trees and

go deeper.
Here, give me your hand."
He looks at me only.
"Let me stay the blood, anyway."
He said in time
it would stop on its own accord.

The first time it happened, Anninho,
my grandmother came to me.
She said that her eyelids were itching
and the back of her tongue
and her private parts were itching.
She turned me around because
she wanted to see my womanhood.
She said now I had my womanhood.
She said that's what she'd been
waiting to see. And then she was
hiding something in me.
Not with her hands; her hands
stayed at her sides.
She was hiding it with her eyes.
She was hiding it deep in me.
She was hiding it deep.

"I spend all my days in tobacco.
Tar on my body.
All this dark tar on my body.
In my clothes.
Staining the soles of my feet,

my toenails. Tobacco spirits."
A tall, weed-long woman in a dress
made of burlap, holes cut
for neck and sleeves.

It is raining in the mountains,
Anninho, and I have the smell
and taste of wet wood.
If you were to kiss me now,
you would draw your tongue away.
It's been a long time since I
had the flesh of a man inside me.
The flesh and feel of a man.
But you bring me more than your flesh;
you brought your blood and spirit, too.
All time is one, Anninho, and I am
the beginning. I am as I was when
you said I was as beautiful as thunder.
"Thunder's not beautiful."
"Have you ever seen thunder?"
"No." I laugh.
"You're as beautiful as your laugh, then.
Are you afraid of thunder?"
"No."
"You're as beautiful as your laugh."

You would draw your tongue away
if you were to kiss me now.
I have the taste of wet wood.

My muscles are still lean,
but I have the taste of wet wood.

I will not prepare myself for men to want me.
My hair will go without oil.
And body will go without oil.
This is not the time for a man.

You're as beautiful as thunder.
I have the taste of wet wood.

This is the wrong time for a man.

The other women were afraid of
the mutilated woman
because she had done what
they would not do.
Yet they called her a coward;
they called her a coward because
she did that evil thing to her body.
They said she was an evil woman
to have done such an evil thing.
Yet some of the others, when it
was their "time," would go to the
"maker of angels" rather than
bring the babe into such an existence.
Eh, it is a world where
the vices and virtues are confused.
It is the same now as then.
Such things do not change.

This is the wrong time.

My grandmama was the only one who would
go near her, and they would
converse of things. My grandmother
regretted that the woman had done
that thing to herself
rather than seek out her powers,
if such a thing was necessary.

I will prepare my body for no man.
This is not the season.
I must await a new season.
I must await a new season
before I will anoint my body for a man.
I must await a new season.
I will anoint my spirit
as well as my flesh then.

"Why do I feel this way, Anninho?"
"What way?"
"This way I feel."
"Perhaps it's your time.
It must be your time."
"Perhaps."

What were you going to tell me, Grandmama.
I don't remember.
You said I would be old enough when you told me.
That one must accept the burden of one's

flesh in this world.
That one must accept the burden of one's spirit.
What else?
Isn't that enough? Don't mock me, child.

Come close to me, Anninho,
and speak to me through a kiss.
Speak to me through a kiss
so that this feeling will leave me.
Speak close to me through a kiss,
so that this feeling will leave me
whole. I want to be left whole.
Come close to me, Anninho, and
speak to me through a kiss,
so that this feeling will leave me.
It is not the time for kisses,
it is the wrong time.
No, Anninho, it must be the time.
I can't stand this feeling.
I saw my grandmother
when the wind blew her dress up
and she had the legs of a young girl.
Her legs were slim, but round
with flesh like a young girl's.
She had globes for knees.
And what else?
Her hair was thick and dark
as in the beginning.
She wanted me to tell her
I had got my womanhood,

that I had caught it
like a small bird,
and held it close.
Then was a time it was not easy to catch
one's womanhood and hold it close.
That was why she would argue with
that woman who had done that thing to herself.
Because she had done it without remorse
and carelessly. Because she had done that thing
so that she could cause no beginnings,
so that she could be the source of
no beginnings. Because she had done
that thing not only to her flesh, but
to her spirit, too. Because she no longer
had the spirit of a woman.
But if I were the age I am now,
I would have disagreed with her.
She did have a woman's spirit.
To me it seemed so.
Leave me be, old woman, she would argue back.
I have chosen a different way from yours.
I cannot give myself to a man in this season.
Believe me, I cannot give myself
over to a man in this season. And besides,
I would not be giving. There is
no such thing as giving these days.
There is no end and no beginning.
Can't you understand that?
No, I'm an old woman, who can't understand.

Even in a time of hardness, I can't understand
why a woman would let the bird go.
I can't understand such a thing.
I am an old woman who can't understand
such a thing. What if Almeyda
were not here, nor my own diamond daughter?
My life would be manioc ashes.
Eh, it would be the same and the same.
I'm part past, but I'm part future, too.

Ah, you're a danger to talk to, said the
mutilated woman.

A danger and an adventure, said my grandmother
with her protective smile.

Come close to me, Anninho, so that
you can speak to me through a kiss.
So that I can lose this feeling I have.

It is a feeling that every woman has
at this time.

No, it is not that feeling.
Come close to me, Anninho, and
speak to me through a kiss, speak
to me so that the feeling will go.

Grandmama said we must bear the burden
of our time, whatever it is,

I told the self-mutilated woman.
She wore armbands, necklaces,
bands on her upper arms,
and on holidays, she drew red and black
lines down her nose and forehead,
around her hairline.

"Don't tell me what that old macumbeiro
said. I've done as hard a thing, harder.
It's not a hard thing to let flesh inside
you, as any woman. Eh, I know."
"You are afraid."
"No."
"Yes."
"No, how can I be afraid, if I did a thing
that could have cost me my life?
This is a time, child . . ."
"I am no child."
"This is a time, young one, when a woman
is worth nothing if her body can't
produce for them, or bear the burden
of their flesh. Not ours. But theirs."
"You are afraid."
"No. You are a child."
"There are no children here."
"Then you are a woman who refuses to
understand a hard thing another woman
has done."
"What is that thing?"
"It is nothing you will want to hear."

"I hear everything."
"Ah, this you won't."

It is like we were together so long, Anninho,
that I can trace every curve of you.
I can feel the soft places and
the firm places. Yes, there were soft places.
Do you think every inch of you was hard?
Is that what a man thinks?
That every inch of him is hard—
his hardness falling into a woman's softness.
Yes, there were soft places.
I remember every curve of your spirit.
The hard and soft places.

I am preparing myself for you, Anninho.
I am anointing every place.
I am anointing.
I am preparing myself
I am anointing my spirit.

Anninho, you pour oil into my hand.
More than I need.
But I use it all, because you have given it,
and I do not wish to waste anything
you have given.

I am preparing myself for you, Anninho.
I am anointing even my spirit.

I have found the house of my spirit,
and I am anointing that house.

"Anninho, what did they do to Zumbi?"
"He had taken ten men with him.
They found them in a certain place.
Zumbi killed the men who would surrender.
This I am told.
I do not know.
I am told that after they killed Zumbi
they cut off his head and put it in
a public place to prove to the others
that he was not immortal."
"Eh, they think that is proof?"

I am preparing myself for you, Anninho.
I am preparing even the place of my spirit.
You pour oil into my hand.
It is me, but my right hand has become you,
just for this moment,
and you are pouring the oil.
I am anointing my spirit.
Can you still feel the curves of me,
even as I still feel the curves of you?

"They put him in a public place
so that we would forget he was immortal.
They thought we would believe as they believe,
that with the stroke of a knife a man
would lose his immortality."

She tells me to watch the parade of women
who have let their bodies be made use of.
She leans on her hoe and tells me
to watch them.
I tell her they cannot help it; it is the time
we are living in. It is the time,
and the others would not have been so lucky
as she was, if they had made their bodies
worthless, they would not have been so lucky.
And why was it the master hadn't killed her?
What was her story?
What was her charm?
"Suppose they had all done what you did?"
She keeps watching. She won't answer.
Her smile is heavy.
Her eyes are hard, on them, and then on me.
"Suppose they had done what you did?"
"Yes, suppose it," is all she will say.
Her eyes are coals.
There's a long mad scar down the side
of her face. It was not there in the beginning.
In the beginning, it was not there.
"Stop watching me."
"What?"
"Stop watching me and be silent.
They think I have mutilated myself, but
I have kept myself whole."
The scar on her face deepens.
Her eyes deepen.
Her eyes go deep in her face.

She is dark.
She is smooth and dark
and her eyes are deep in her face.

"Anninho."
"Hush, woman. Or speak quieter.
Here we must whisper.
There are ears all places."

Those birds. It was like they were
calling each other. No talking.
One of their voices was lower than
the other. One would give two
sounds and then the other three,
or the first one would give one sound
and the other three or four. No,
I don't know what kind of birds
they were but they would vary it
like that. I could tell how you felt then.
Your eyes got deeper and you looked at
me the way I had not seen you look
at any other woman. Your eyes got deeper.
They got so deep in your face, Anninho.

"Why didn't you speak to me, woman?
You saw me and didn't speak."
"Because I."
"Why?"
"Nothing."

"What, woman?"
"You will say it is not the time.
It is time that we move on.
It is time that we picked up our burdens
and moved on."
"What?"
"Kiss me. Just here. On my forehead. Yes.
That's what I wanted to tell you then.
No, it was like I had no words for you
and I was afraid to look at you,
and when I did, there was that thing
in your eyes and you hadn't looked
at any other woman that way. No other woman.
No man has eyes like you.
All that darkness."
"No woman has eyes like you.
The way your eyes have taken over your face."
"All that darkness I was going to say.
And how far they go.
How far back they go, like a deep well.
How far I feel they can see,
and how far back they go.
A woman would have to paint dark lines
around her eyes to get them just that way."
"Why didn't you speak to me?"
"Because I was afraid to. Because I was afraid
you wouldn't have felt what I was feeling."
"And when you found out I did?"
"I had nothing to fear then."

I dreamed that King Zumbi came to me, Anninho,
robed in all his immortality,
and he was glowing.

You are the man that came between
the wind and me, Anninho.
I had nothing to fear.
Where are my breasts?
Where is my necklace of shells and seeds?
That soldier, Anninho,
he tore my necklace of shells and seeds
away and then he tore my breasts away.
I am confused about that time,
and now I seek you again,
and you are somewhere seeking me.
Ah, if we could have and keep each other.
Ah, for the new time and the New Palmares.
"What are they?"
"Pomegranate seeds and trumpet shells."

He came to me, Anninho, in all of his
immortality, he told me what you told me,
that men like those do not understand how
flesh and blood and spirit continue in the world.
Where is my woman?
I don't know, King Zumbi.
Where is my dream?
I told him it was inside me, Anninho,
but, in truth, I was always too much in awe

of King Zumbi to speak to him.
Always I saw him from a distance.
But even from a distance,
when he was talking to all the people,
his spirit captured me and held till he
was done talking, and beyond talk.
I do not know even if he knew that such
a woman as Almeyda existed among the
thousands who lived in the quilombos.
I always saw him from a distance,
and when he spoke, I'd give careful ear
to his laws, religious and secular,
his solemn intelligence. You knew him
up close because you sat on the council,
and were in charge of trading and
reconnaissance expeditions for him.
Ah, how his spirit captured me and held me.
"Did you ever wish you were Zumbi's woman
and not mine?"
"No."
"Still he comes into your dreams."
"How can such a man not come into
everyone's dreams? It is not a case
for jealousy. Such a sun must shine."
He smiles. "I am not jealous.
Even in his presence I stayed in awe of him.
I loved him dearly. How could one not love
such a leader? Ah, what would the world
be like, if he had not been captured?

They put him in the most public place
of Recife. Do they think that his spirit
won't return? He was the only man I ever
stood in awe of. In the New Palmares,
we'll maintain his codes and discipline,
and in that way he'll be there.
We'll write his chronicles in wars against
them, and in the settling of accounts.
Ha. They think they can kill his immortality.
While I'm out writing his chronicles in
expeditions against the Portuguese,
you'll stay in the new place, writing
his chronicles to hold against theirs.
You see how they transform heroes into villains,
and noble actions into crimes, and elevated
codes into venality?"
"I'll write *your* chronicles, Anninho."
He laughs.
"But it's not the actions I wish to capture,
but the spirit!"
He laughs again and kisses my forehead.

2.

"He tore my necklace of seeds."
"Who?"
"A soldier. One of them."
"He had no name?"
"No. For me he had no name.
It is only you and the Palmaristas
who have names for me. In my chronicles,
not even their military chieftains will
have names. There's no such one as Velho,
there's no such one as Furtado do Mendoca
in the world! There are only Zumbi,
and Anninho, and Ganga Zumba and . . ."
"Ganga Zumba was a traitor."
"Even our traitors have names.
But there is no one such as Velho!"
"But in denying their names,
you have given them names."

"What is your name?"
"Almeyda."

The Portuguese soldier tore my necklace
of seeds and shells and then he cut

off my breasts. He was without a name,
as I had no name for him.
This is an age that doesn't allow names,
Anninho, only eyes.
All kinds of eyes.
All kinds of eyes, everything in them
but tenderness.
No place for tenderness.
Anger, hardness, madness only.

"What kind of seeds?"
"I don't know their names."
"Can they be eaten?"
"Yes. Didn't you know that
in this world
anything can be eaten?"

And the love songs, Anninho.
Sing me a love song.
At first I thought it was an
age when we must leave the love songs behind,
or get new voices to
sing them.

In a new voice or the old one,
we must make our love songs.
Hear the birds.
They are making a racket, aren't they?
They are all singing together.
They are trying to sing in one voice,

but one discordant voice,
one voice with many variations.
It is a difficult song they are singing.
It hurts my ears to hear them.
Why are they all trying to sing at once?
Why don't they let me sleep,
just get a little sleep before we start
the long walk? This is the
kind of voice that can tear dreams apart
and make new ones.

"We must remake our voices, Anninho.
This is an age when the old voices won't do."
"Sing me a love song."
"My voice is not ready."
"When will it be ready?"
"I don't know."
"Sing me a love song."
"I must wait."
"Why should you be ashamed to sing to me?
It's the others that should have been ashamed."
"Yes."
"It is the others that should have covered
themselves in shame. Not our women."

I remember when we came to each other,
and we both had heavy smiles, Anninho,
because this was not the time or place
for a man and woman, and so we bore heavy
smiles, it was no time for an easy smile,

and we came together without speaking,
because there were no words for such a time,
and we would not have known each other's
voices even if we had spoken. It was a time
when a man and woman could not recognize
each other's voices. Recognition came only
with a way of touching, a smell, and even
that was heavy and full of sweat. But we
recognized each other and we were somehow
smiling. We tightened our lips together
and our blood became one, our sweat became
one.
"Always wear your hair that way."
"Do you like it?"
Hand on my waist.
Speak to me so close with a kiss.
I will make all my laughter a love song,
but it can only be a heavy laughter,
a laughter that takes up the sounds of
things I am not telling you, it can only
be that kind of laughter. And all those
things, Anninho, all those things my mouth
wouldn't form.
"Watch out here."
He takes my arm.
"Are you frightened?"
"No."
"Be careful. Don't fall."
"No."
"You're OK?"

"Yes."

Oh, our smiles were so heavy and we could
both feel that thing weighing our insides.
We could both feel it.

He made her naked.

*Yes, I saw him undress her and she held her
hands out like flowers.*

Now I must have a double vision, Anninho,
I must be alone here and still see us
doing those beautiful things.

*A man wants to be able to take a woman
someplace anyplace and not just a place
inside a dream either but a place hard with
reality and desire.*

"My ankles are paining."

"We'll stop here."

"No."

"I said we'll stop."

There is a cool wind near this river.
You have your hands on my wrists and
my wrists are throbbing.

"There was something we forgot back there."

"What?"

"I don't remember."

"I don't remember either."

And it is a time when you can't go back
for the things, you must remember everything
with your blood because you can't go back
for them.

"Your forehead is full of ditches, Anninho.

There is grass sticking to your hair."
I stand near the river, the place where
the mud is soft. I walk without any shoes.
"Come on."
He is watching me.
"I'm coming."
You're a woman now, Almeyda.
Yes. I'm still riding beneath your shoulders.
Come and dance.
This is no time. The mud here is too soft.
No place you mean.
No. No time.
"We'll have to go farther in this way.
Your eyes are sad, woman. There was only
one time I saw them light up and your dreams
were as large as life."
"Our life now?"
"Any life."
My smile then was as heavy as life.
And you kept putting seeds
and shells in my hands, telling me
to put them in a safe place and you would
string them later.
It has been years since I knew what a man was like.
What?
I said it's been years since the flesh of a man
flowed into me. And since that river of blood
stopped and the big wound closed.
What?

Never mind.
From where?
Can't you see without my telling?
I wanted my womb to grow deep for you, Anninho,
even in a time like this one,
in spite of the time. I wanted my womb
to grow deeper than the earth.
I wanted my womb to grow deeper
than the earth. But my womb was angry.
Maybe time made my womb.
Maybe the times.
And then that bitterness sucked my womb dry.
I opened my legs and you touched me,
not saying anything.
I felt the heaviness of bread soaked in water.

There is a cool wind blowing near this river.
You hold my breasts and my breasts are throbbing.
"Did you feel the wind? There's a cool wind now."
"Yes."
"It's a good feeling."

"You should always wear your hair that way."
"You're making fun of me."
"No."
He keeps watching me. His smile is heavy.
I think of the time we decorated our house
with banana leaves and flowers,
preparing our wedding; and the long private

time afterwards. But outside the blacksmiths
were still making weapons, and the woodcarvers
carving pointed sticks and new fences.
"The wind is cool here, Anninho; can we stand
here a moment?"
He slows down, then stops. It is a short moment
we stand there. He keeps his back to me, then
we start up again.
"It won't be good to stand longer than this,"
he says, and then we move on.
I watch his back. If it was a different time,
I could relax in my watching. It is a tense
watching. We walk through a tunnel of trees.

Do you remember the night, Anninho,
that we could raise the moon upon our shoulders?
That night we lifted up the moon, and carried it
on our shoulders. We lifted it up out of the river,
and onto the mountain, and then onto our shoulders.
The sun had just gone down, full of blood,
but we lifted the moon up on our shoulders.

I feel myself a long way away from you.
Why?
It is when I start to remember certain things,
some things pull me close and other things throw me
away from you.

You hold my wrists and my wrists become my heart.

Everything happens again. There is nothing
in this world that doesn't happen again.

I felt that my own eyes had gotten deeper
and that I went to the bottom of them.
I dwelt at the bottom of my own eyes.
That was what I did when there was no place
else for me to go and dwell.

"Are you thirsty?"
"Yes."
"Drink from this."
"The water here is as thick as mud."

And if I sang you a love song now,
Anninho, it would be the kind that would
hurt your ears. It would set your ears
to bleeding. I would have to change my voice.
I would have to make a new voice,
and it would be a difficult voice.
It would not be romantic.
It would be full of desire without
possibility. It would not be like
the old songs, Anninho. It would be
like none of the old songs.
"There are no new songs."
"Yes, I heard a new song. An old man was singing it.
Yesterday."
"It was an old song repeated forever."
"No. A new one. He said it was a new one."

"No. He was an old man. He had lost his memory.
It came from the same well as all the others.
He had forgotten.
He was old and had lost his memory,
and so he thought it was new."
"I will create a new one."
"Maybe."
"Ah, let me sing this love song, old or new."

Old man, go over the words again.
You should have heard them the first time.
I did hear.
Remember them then. This is an age when
all we have is our memories.
Oh? And you have lost yours.
Sing me a love song.
I don't know you.
Does it matter?
You're an old man.
Does it matter?

"Anninho, my breasts are swelling.
I feel them swelling.
They are gone but I feel them swelling.
It is cold in the mountains
this time of year. It seeps into me.
It seeps through my sleeves,
and this old fortune teller is curing me,
with leaves and water and persuasion.
I am bread soaked in milk.

Sing me a love song.
I've forgotten all the words.
Then hum them.
The tune is lost to me.
Then come close to me and kiss me.

It is cold in these mountains.
It is a new season,
and a fortune teller tells me
that I must search for you,
as if the first finding was not sufficient.

"Thunder."
"What?"
"Your beauty is like thunder."

My breasts are heavy, Anninho, and she is curing me.
I am bread soaking in milk.
She says my breasts were globes floating
in the river, and that it is only
memory and desire that replace them;
make them feel heavy.
I tell her we are both lovers of riding,
and when I find you, we'll go riding
through these mountains, whether it's
against the law or not for a black man and woman
to be seen on horseback.
At the New Palmares, we'll
trade manioc and hide
for horses, and ride through these mountains.

"Do you see the light through the trees?"
"Yes."
"It's nice."
"Yes."
"It looks like the sun is rising from that tree."

That time before we were together, Anninho,
I felt you looking at me and when I looked at you,
you looked away. And then I looked away.

"Do you see the sun through the trees?"
"Yes."

It is cold in these mountains in this season.
The cold has come early this season.

When there is no other place, Anninho,
that is when I dwell at the bottom of my eyes.
Not mine?
I wanted to go there, Anninho.

"We must find a place before dark.
There is no moon.
I know this kind of darkness well.
It is the kind where not even the face
of the woman you love can be seen.
There is no moon to heave onto the shoulders.
We must find a place for the night.
The moon is in the ocean."

Did you see the eyes of that woman?
Yes, I saw them.

"What will become of us, Anninho?"
He doesn't answer, then he says,
"Do you believe me about this darkness?"
"Yes. Because I cannot see the face of
the man I love in it."
"And more?"
"No."
"I can feel the thickness of your hair,
and how your blood rushes into mine."
"How far do we have to go?"
"One never knows. One knows only how to say
we will camp here and when the night is finished,
one knows only how to say, Get to your feet again."

Zumbi brought the one with the light skin and fair
hair among us and they called her the Reina Blanca,
the daughter of some forest dweller, her hair
clean and long.

"We must find a place, for I know this kind
of darkness."

The women are different, the men tell us,
the women become a part of whatever people
they come among. It does not matter if
the woman is blanca or negra, women are different,

they become wherever they are. She's from one
of the forest families we trade with. Women are
different. It does not matter.

Do you remember the words to the love song?
No; how do you expect me to remember?
I am an old woman who forgets such things.
You have not forgotten.
I have forgotten.
You play games.
She has spread a blanket and she sits on it.
She covers her feet with the end of the blanket.
For her, it is a sin to show one's feet.
Especially it is not right for a man to see
one's feet.
She picks out the mud and rubs it in her hair.
She says it will make her hair grow.
She says her hair has lost the thickness
it had when she was a young woman.
She keeps the blanket on her feet.
She is ashamed to show her feet.
It is the young ones who show their feet.

"One never knows. One knows only how to say we
will camp here and when the night is finished, one
knows only how to say, Get to your feet again."

The women are different. We know about the women.
It does not matter. Women are always to be taken
in wars of liberation. Call her the Reina Blanca.

It does not matter with a woman. They are always
captured when there is the need. They forget
where they were and become where they are.
Not true.
Tell me what then,
It is the women always who are spared, only that.
You know why.
I have known women who have not been spared,
It is because they have shown, somehow shown themselves
dangerous.

In the morning, there are crows under my eyes.
"Your eyes are dark."
"Yes."
But I stand with my bundle. He kicks his with
his feet, then picks it up.

I step in and outside memory, Anninho.
I am one of those who forgets what time
they are in.

Yes, I lived with him because in those days
we were the women they wanted. Do not condemn me.
There was no choice then. There is no choice now.
It is a miracle that you have had a choice.
That you have had the man you desired in the beginning.
That is something. To have a choice in a season
of no choices.
Yes.

"Can you see me?"

"Yes."

"The day is breaking through the trees."

"A different day, but the same time."

I hug my knees. I hug my knees to me.

The fortune teller/healer tells me that I

must go on a long journey in search of you.

I am bread soaking in milk and beeswax and honey.

Look at me, woman.

What?

Look at me, I said.

I am looking.

Anninho's eyes go deeper. He pulls me inside them.

I do not refuse to go. I do not refuse to go

into his eyes because he is the man I

wanted to stay with. I wanted to stay with that man.

I wanted to stay with him.

Look at me.

I am.

I saw him look at me, fortune teller, wizard woman,

old stargazer, but I wasn't looking then and when I

looked at him, he had already turned away. Yes,

it was in the corner of my eyes that I saw him.

"Anninho."

He turns back. This is the turning with all love in it.

This is the turning.

"It is a long journey, Almeyda."
"I know."
"You must create the roads as you travel them."
"I know."

These people they do not understand.
They think they are responsible
only to what they do in this time.
They are responsible to all time.

"Do you fear me?"
"No."

Rain. Rain that goes through the clothes,
that goes clear through to the marrow.

"Couldn't you tell by my eyes that
I wanted to be with you?"
"No. It's hard to tell with a woman like you."

It goes clear to the marrow, this rain.

Anninho, I saw you walking in the distance,
but I could not go to you for I was with
the other women. I was in a circle of women,
and for that reason I did not go to you.
Everyone was in the circle, except Zumbi's women,
talking about what it was like to be treated
with dignity again. Even the Indian women
had joined us, sharing the same feeling,

165

sharing secrets with us,
bringing each other out of despair,
cutting down forests of despair,
celebrating the new women.

I was in a circle of women, and I could not
go to you. We were mending straw mats,
and cutting down forests.
I could not go to you then.

Now I am sitting with my knees drawn up,
my arms wrapped around my knees.
If it were now, I would get up.
If it were now, I would rise up and go to you.
That is what I would do if it were
in this time.
But then I would not go.
I was afraid.
I was afraid of the other women's eyes.
I was afraid of their voices.
They had strong eyes and voices.
And anyway, wasn't it a significant thing
we were doing?
And you were standing with the men, watching.
But if it were now.
If it were in this time.
If it were now,
I would have gone to you.
I would have left the circle of women.
I would have left the straw mats.

I would have left the celebration.
But then was the wrong time.
I was one of the new ones,
and you could not have helped me
with that forest.
I needed their conversation,
but your presence.
We were talking about what it was like
to be treated with dignity again.
When the time came,
I rose and stood near you.

This is not the time for a man.
We create our times.

"What do you want from me, Anninho?"
"Your being."
His being and my being.
Love in such a time
becomes that.

Now in this time, Anninho,
I must go on a long journey
to reclaim you.

"Come on, Almeyda. Let's take a walk."
And I go with him.

All time is raw.
Things change and change.

I am restless. I walk.
The mosquitoes take as much blood
now as they ever did.

Love heals, says the curador.

I did not know what kind of love song
I would sing,
until I sang it.

I am restless. I walk.
"A woman wishing a certain man were here,"
says the curador from the doorway.

When I walk, I still feel my forehead
resting against my knees.
There is a raw scar where my breasts were.
I remember the soldier without a name.
Stone cups in a granary.

I saw your smile. I looked at you.
You weren't looking at me then,
but you were smiling.

Come on, Almeyda. Don't you want to come with me?
Yes, I want to come.

When will it be time for us, Anninho and I?
I asked the curador.

I have told you of your journey, she tells me.
I cannot tell you beyond that.
You must teach yourself where you must go.

She looks at me.

I see him. I see his eyes mostly.
Time and distance are always the bridge.

"Do you not regret sometimes?" I asked
the self-mutilated woman.
"No."
"Never?"
"No."
"You have not wanted?"
"No. Yes, there are times. I feel as full
of despair as any woman."
"You have had a man?"
"He came and went."
"Talk about him."
"No."
"Was he one of them?"
"One of us."
"Talk about him."
"No."
"And so you did that thing so that you would not have
to bear the burden of your time."
"So that I *would*."

What did we say in the beginning?
It was something that was
said way back in the beginning, Anninho.
What was said was said
in the beginning.
And the words
made me throw my arms up with joy.
The words made me throw my arms up.
That joy made me throw my arms up.

Desire is real.
A leaf twisted in a palm.

"Almeyda, why don't you speak?"
"Because there is too much to say
right now, Anninho. Too
much to say. We must go back to the
beginning to say it all,
and even then it will not be said."

Surrounded by forest,
I dream of thick walls of buildings
anointed with whale oil.
I dream of buildings
and the touch of hands.
I am in the
small room in the center
of one of the houses.
I am in the inner room.

"Why won't you sing to me, Almeyda?"
"I fear the words won't come as I mean them."
"Let the words come anyway."

I saw two animals.
They were the same kind of animal,
two squirrels, I think, or field rats,
and one started chasing the
other one. But there was no place
that one could go that the
other one couldn't go.
One started up the tree,
but the other one followed,
and they kept circling,
but it was bad because
there was no place that one could go
that the other one couldn't follow.
That was the bad thing.
They were the same size,
so why was it that one chased
and the other ran?
I kept wondering why the other one
couldn't have turned and run
after *that* one.
Why couldn't that one have turned around
and done the chasing?
Was it sexual?
No.
There are no birds. All day there have been birds.

But right now I can hear no birds'
voices. There. That's one.
There. There are the birds.
Yes, I thought they would
come back, because all day
there have been birds.

"What were you doing with her? I saw you
standing with her, Anninho."
"Who?"
"The woman who mutilated herself. The woman
who had done that thing to herself.
The woman who wanted no man."
"It was a dream."
"No. I saw you. And you were talking close
to her. You were talking close.
You were talking close
the way you talked to me in the beginning."
"You were jealous."
"Yes."
"We were only talking, and what's the harm
in that? She was telling me that if she
had seen Palmares in her future,
she would never have done that thing.
But she had seen no possibility or choice
and so had done it out of the spirit's conviction.
Let the woman talk to me.
What's the harm?"
"What else did you speak of?"

"Questions of faith and the latest raids."
"What else did you speak of?"
He doesn't answer. He kisses me and we go
into our house and eat cassava and rice.

What else did you speak of?
People and time.

"He brought the one with the fair skin
and the long hair among us."
"Who?"
"*He* did. He brought her around us
and when it was time for the dance,
he chose her. There she was
shaking her long hair. What can
you do when there's a fair-skinned
woman with long hair among you?
What do you do?"

It was in those days, Anninho,
Grandmother said, that everyone wanted
a woman from the coast.
They had let the Indian women go
and wanted an intelligent woman from the coast.

"What do you do when there's
a woman with long hair among you?"

I saw you standing close to her, Anninho.
I saw you.

And my heart was balled up like a fist.
I wasn't jealous.
No.
But my heart, Anninho.
My heart became my whole body.
But I let the woman talk to you.

"What is wrong with you, woman?"
"Nothing."
"Why did you wait so long?"
"I thought it was the wrong time."
"And you thought this would be a better one?"
"No."
"Woman."
"What?"
"Why did you wait so long to come to me?"
"It was the wrong time.
But is it important?
Is it important how long?
Isn't it important that I came?"

Didn't I let her talk to you?
Even if she had done that thing to her own self,
I could see in her eyes and lightning smile—
the blood rushing to the continent on her forehead.
Ah, I could see.
Ah, if she had not done that thing to herself
Ah, if she had known there was a future.
A woman of passion still,
and love transcending time.

But I let her talk.

And what happened to the Indian woman?
She is still here.
And me?
You have come.
Have I taken her place?
She is still here, I said.
And the other?
What other?
The fair-skinned one. The woman
with the long hair. When will she come?
But she cannot survive here.
Who?
The fair-skinned one.
You are jealous.
No. It is those who come from us who will survive.
And you?
This land is not different from my home. I will survive.
But you are jealous.
No.

I can put centuries of any feeling
into one moment, if I choose.

Speak to me softly and close through a kiss, Anninho.
And we will have our time of tenderness.
We will make our time of tenderness.

We will make that time.
Centuries of loving in that moment.

I saw her watching me.
Who?
The fair-skinned woman. And he had drawn
a picture of a woman. I saw it.
He gave the woman her long hair and my dark skin
and eyes.
Did you love him?
But that is a legacy of history, an enchantment
of history.
Yes, I said.
And you understand everything.
No. I try to understand.

"What is it?"
"Nothing."
"You said you would come with me."
"Yes."
"Are you afraid?"
"No."

She must have seen the picture, too.
Who?
The other woman, the fair-skinned one.
What do you mean?
She began to make her skin dark. She stayed in
the sun and made her skin darker, but there was
no way in the world I could make my hair long
and dark and flowing like hers. She could fulfill
the enchantment more easily than I. The legends
of enchanted Moorish women bathing in fountains.

It was mulatto women he wanted, I say.
It was his own daughter he wanted then—
neither you nor her.

The birds are back, Anninho.
Yes.
They are singing in one voice.

What do you want? That is one fat hard question.
It is a question a woman asks a man, and a man a woman.
What do you want? What is it?

They are singing in one voice, Anninho.
They are singing in one tight, careful voice.

"You are good to me."
"What?"
But I don't say it again.

That woman went where the sun was hottest,
so she could make her skin darker.
So she could make her skin dark like the
Moorish woman in the fountain.
The enchanted Moorish woman her husband had drawn.
Neither me nor her. But an enchantment she could manage.
The Moorish woman combing her hair out, oiling it.

This is a time when you could have been hard with me.
You could have been hard with me.
But no, you came gently, touching

my shoulders, my eyes, all my feelings.
You could have come swollen with anger and hard.
You could have brought the pain with you,
but I knew the pain, too. There was no need to
bring it. And you emptied my fear from my belly.
This is a time when you could have been excused
for your hardness, but you refused to be hard.
You emptied my belly of fear.
You gave me long moments of tenderness.
In the beginning, I wondered what it was you wanted
with me? Why it was me that you had chosen.
Why it was me you spoke close to with a kiss.
Why it was my flesh and blood and spirit you chose?

"Are you cold?"
"No."
"You said you were cold before."
"You know it does not get cold in this part
of the country."
"It was all feeling, then?"
"Yes, it was all feeling."

"You have been good to me, Anninho."
He says nothing, but I like what he has
in his eyes for me in this moment.

In the beginning, Anninho, a man and woman
spoke close to each other, through a kiss,
and all the pain and anger and fear

were lost in that moment. They exposed
themselves to each other and held each other up,
heavy and laughing, and were happy in that moment.
Will it come again?
Yes.

"But you young ones, you young ones have
lost your tenderness, have forgotten the
tender ways. You refuse to go on the long
hunt for the ways a man must be with a woman,
the ways a woman must be with a man. It is
a long and difficult hunt, a journey you
refuse to go on."
"Did you refuse?"
"Can't you tell by my eyes?"
"What did you find?"
There is still no answer. She asks her eyes
to tell, but they are telling nothing.

My whole being is a fist. My whole being
is drawn up tight like a fist.
My soul is a fist.

What brings us together in this place?

The porcupine had no meat, only quills,
and we had to hold the quills in our teeth.
But there was nothing to suck out.
There was nothing in them to suck out.

Quills, and the bones were without marrow,
and so there was nothing, not anything
to suck from the bones.

What about the man whose eyes you remember?
Did you want him?

Yes.

But you wouldn't?

No.

Who was he?

I remember only his eyes.

3.

Anninho, the muscles in my belly have tightened
like parched leather.

In the beginning, there was only your kiss.

In the beginning, there was only your kiss, Anninho.

He keeps watching my face.

What is it, woman? Are you lonely?

No.

In the beginning was only your kiss, Anninho.

Answer again.

About what?

Your loneliness.

Yes.

You were standing close to her, Anninho,
asking her if she was lonely. It is okay.
Talk to her.

She has done that horror to herself. The
horror so that no man would take her, before
she knew there was a future. So stand close
to her, if you wish. Kiss her. The long kiss
that heals, or that persuades healing. I'll
not swallow porcupine quills because you've
spoken quietly with her, too. I'll watch her
eyes soften. I'll pick my teeth with a
porcupine quill.

In the beginning was your kiss, Anninho.

And he was dancing with the long-haired one and her
hair was falling down around her feet and she had
made herself dark like me. He sent to the old country
or her. Portugal. And then when she came, she saw
how he behaved about dark women. And her arms were
up in the air and she was dancing, trying to dance
like we dance, like she thought we dance. He had
sent for her, and she hated the dark women. She'd
made herself dark like us, but she hated us.

I let you speak to her, the self-mutilated woman,
and even kiss her, Anninho. A ritual of healing.

Are you hungry?

No.

He put his hand on the back of my neck.

Don't draw away. Are you afraid of me?

No.

Do you feel the same way I do?

Yes.

I was a bell, in those days.

His hand on the back of my neck, he drew me
close to him.

I wanted you to hold me this way in the beginning.

He drew me close, and I met the new day.

And we are moving again through tall trees.

We left the others, Anninho, and we went on
the long journey through the tall trees,
and now she asks me to go on another journey,
the sun rising and setting. Then your back was
always in front of me, and we walked,

183

and I remained close to you. And the mud was
deep, or the land was hard and dry, and I
remained close. And we were saying nothing.
And I felt heavy. And there were no words.
And I was heavy. And when we would come to
a place of rest, you put your hand on the back
of my neck and pulled me inside you. And now,
I must go on another journey, this time to seek you.

We are the same blood, Anninho.

Yes.

We are the same blood.

Yes.

We are the same blood.

Yes.

What became of *him? Zumbi.*

*They killed him so that his people would not
think he was immortal.*

*I saw his eyes. He had the eyes of an
immortal man.*

I wonder how his woman feels.

You know how she feels.

Yes.

And I dreamed that the white long-haired women
danced around the head of Zumbi. The men had
put Zumbi's head on a pole, and the women came
raising their skirts and falling sometimes to
the ground in their dancing. They danced
patting their bellies and spreading their legs
apart, and they had made themselves dark like
our women. They had burned their skins dark.
They had found a day that was hot and bleeding
and stretched themselves out on the ground and
burned their skins dark.

Where are the colored women? They said there
were colored women dancing around the head of Zumbi.

No, these are not colored women. They found
a day that was bleeding and hot, and made themselves
dark, and pretended.

Are these colored women?

No.

His eyes are immortal.

They expose their pubic parts to his immortal eyes.
The meat there is still white.

How is the look of immortality?

It is one of gentleness. His eyes were gentle.
But it was a piercing gentleness. It was a
gentleness that cuts through to the soul. And as
he watched them, his eyes pierced through to the
bone, and to the marrow in the bone.

One woman brought him a pomegranate, split it open.
The seeds of the pomegranate are covered with blood.
She raised one half to his mouth, the other to hers.

Is this a colored woman?

No, I tell you. She has made her skin dark
and her eyes big with charcoal and licorice.

Kiss me, Almeyda.
I kiss without words.

The other women, their breasts are buckets that
they fill with something heavy and red.

Whose woman are you?

I am Anninho's woman.

For how long?

From the beginning.

Nonsense. How long?

In the beginning, I was his.

Are you a colored woman?

No. I am the granddaughter of an African.

You are a colored woman, then.

They were dancing. They were raising their skirts
and putting themselves close to him. They wanted
his eyes to swallow them whole.

Where are the colored women?

They are there. Over there.

I want that one.

I am Anninho's woman.

I want the bitch with the charcoal eyes. Yes,
that one.

I have become this landscape. My legs open are
two of its rivers.

Are you one of the master's bastard children?

No. I am the granddaughter of an African.
And there are no bastards here.

She split the pomegranate open and lifted half to
his face. He did not eat of it. The seeds of the
pomegranate are covered with flesh. She bit into
the part she had kept for herself.

Where are the bastard children, then?

There are none here.

Zumbi's eyes watch the two of us, for we have come
and chased those women away, and we stand before
Zumbi, and he is glad we have come.

Talk to me, Almeyda.

Yes, I am. I am talking.

The sweet rain has come and my breasts turn into
buckets, and I cannot get enough of this rain.

Where are your breasts?

The soldier cut them.

You are beautiful.

Those words belong to other women.

You are beautiful, Almeyda.

I must speak with you, Anninho. There is something
I must say.

What is it, woman?

But we were sitting close together then. Anninho,
we were so close and there was only that way you were
looking at me.

Do you want me to come with you?

Yes.

There was only that way, Anninho, and that moment
we had made.

Do you want me to say something?

No.

You had made yourself a cigarette. You went away
and came back and sat near me. I watched you,
and found some deep place in you where I could go
any moment.

Now I make roads for you, Anninho. I make roads.

—Almeyda, Barriga Mountains, 1697

189